Tiger's Adventures *in the* Everglades

VOLUME FOUR

As told by T. F. Gato

jay gee heath

ALSO BY JAY GEE HEATH

Mystery/Romance
Right Talents
Right Skills
Right Dreams
Right Response
Right Target
Right Solution
Right Villain

Tiger
Tiger's Adventures in the Everglades
Tiger's Adventures in the Everglades Volume Two
Tiger's Adventures in the Everglades Volume Three

Joyce G Heath

ISBN 978-1-7371449-2-2 paperback
ISBN 978-1-7371449-3-9 ebook

Second edition

Publisher
Joyce G. Heath
jaygeeheath@yahoo.edu
jaygeeheath@gmail.com

DEDICATION

To Sam

ACKNOWLEDGEMENT

Janet Benjamins
Jo Anne Sullivan
Jean Smith

Cover cat and Art by K. T. Gato

Yes there really was a Tiger. And, yes, he had adventures in the Everglades. These stories are based on those two facts with fiction so thoroughly intertwined that even the author is no longer sure which is fact and which is fiction.

Princess, the Siamese cat with the leg and tail stripes, was real. You can thank Grant and The Rock for her inclusion.

CONTENTS

LIST OF ART

CUMBERLAND ISLAND

How dare she? How could she? She put me into this stupid cage again. She's supposed to carry me on her shoulder, not put me in a stupid cage. Then she put the stupid cage on the stupid boat. Just plonked the stupid cage down on the deck beside a duffel bag, a suitcase, and supplies for the island. What does that make me?

Argh. I can't even see anything. My view is blocked.

The boat engines start with a loud roar and we are on our way to Cumberland Island National Seashore off Georgia's coast. I don't even know Georgia, but that's where Boston said we are going. To visit Pete and Carla for a day. I know them. They give me treats. They transferred from the Everglades last year and are caretaking the Carnegie Mansion, Plum Orchard.

Boston shouldn't treat me like baggage. I'm a Maine Coon cat after all. Well, almost a Coon cat, near enough. Not some dumb suitcase. No one can see me hidden with the supplies and no one can hear me over the whine of the engine. I can't stop my lip from curling or the snarl. For all the good it does me. But it makes me feel a little better.

I can't hear anything but the stupid engine. The whole boat shakes. And each time we hit a wave my cage bounces.

Finally, finally, the engine sound moderates and then stops. The shaking stops too. My lady lifts my cage to the dock, cooing at me as if that will make it okay. I'm so mad I'm not even going to look at her, but she opens the door, pulls me out, and sets me up on her shoulder. Stroking me.

"Don't sulk, kitty," she begs.

Why not? You shoved me in that cage, treated me like luggage. It is a nice enough cage. Kevlar built it for her. For me. Looks like a long igloo, made of screen on a wood frame. So I can see out all around if I am not blocked by stupid supplies. It has my pillow in the bottom. And a couple of toys.

True, if she had tried holding me in her arms to carry me onto the stupid boat, I wouldn't have let her. She probably knew that. Even so.

She is stroking me and talking. "We're going to ride in an electric car. Say hi to Pete; he's driving." Pete shakes hands with Kevlar, gives her a half hug around me, "Welcome to Cumberland, Boston." He taps my head. He is not a cat person. I move my head away from a second tap. He smells of cigarette smoke.

Kevlar puts my cage and their duffle and the suitcase in the cart and gets in front with Pete. Me and Boston get the back seat The cart is open. I get to ride in an open car. Yea.

Pete tells us, "Cumberland is a barrier island of dunes, forests, and lakes. Surrounded by beach."

Curious, I look around. Hey, I can sulk and still be interested in my surroundings.

Oops. Water? I am on my lady's right shoulder. Water is on her left. We have water at home. I like to know where it is so I can keep an eye on it. I don't trust it. I'm not afraid of water, just a little edgy around it ever since I almost drowned. But I am nervous and cling a little too tightly to Boston.

"Ouch," she says and pulls one claw out of her arm. But I should be safe with her between me and the ocean.

Pete takes us on a short tour down a crushed shell road. Green vegetation borders my side, and I can see birds flitting quickly through the trees, hmm. No squirrels. Pete points out the ruins of an old crumbling building. "Dungeness. Burned in nineteen-fifty-nine, before Park Service bought most of the land from the Carnegies in seventy-two," he says. "I'll take you on a tour later. Probably not safe for the cat, though."

What do you mean? Cats go into unsafe places all the time. Chasing rats and stuff.

We continue the drive along the shoreline and Pete points out the mud flats, oceanside and some really big four-legged guys. "Feral horses, wild," Pete says as we stop to watch.

I've never seen horses. It's a kick. I saw deer once on a trip out of the park to town. They were not as tall as these guys which makes them kind of scary. Can they see their feet? What if one stepped on me? And what's feral?

"The Spaniards who settled here first brought them.

Domesticated then, but wild now. The Native Americans brought more, and the British did too. They built plantations and harvested sea island cotton and timber. We'll see more horses later. And deer."

We reach the drive to the house and Pete stops to give us the full effect. The house is huge. White. Two story entrance with four pillars. The front porch is longer than our old trailer, the Silver Bullet. The crushed shell road wraps around a wide lawn in front of the house.

"That is beautiful," Boston says. "The live oaks scattered out front, draped with Spanish moss."

There are strange animals moving on the grass. Birds? Yes. I nod my head. They are birds. Big fat squat boring brown birds. Scratching around in the grass. Not the slender graceful birds of the Everglades. Slender, like me. I gather myself to jump down and investigate, but Boston holds me tighter. Two birds face off at each other. They drop their wings low and fan their tails. Short, squat tails. They look a little silly. They have something red and ugly hanging from their chins, ah, beaks. Never seen anything like it.

I move a little, but Boston still has a tight grip. "Wild turkeys," she says.

"Feral turkeys," Pete adds.

Turkeys? Only turkey I've ever seen is the one on the dinner table. Also brown, but glazed not feathered, and it didn't look like these.

"We can't shoot them for Thanksgiving dinner because we are a Designated Wilderness Area," Pete complains.

I can almost see one on the platter, my eyes glass over. How long before I can get free?

Pete says, "They're scratching for food. They prefer this time of day to early evening when the wild pigs, boars, come out."

Bores? The wild pigs are boring?

"Wild pigs? Boars?" Kevlar asks. "Native?"

"Feral also. Brought in by humans. Wild now. Can't say I'm not tempted to put a fine ham and turkey dinner together."

Yum. Sounds like a good idea to me and I try to get loose, but Boston holds me tighter.

"No hunting, Tiger."

Pete continues down the drive to the front door; the cart engine is so quiet we don't disturb the birds or maybe they are used to it coming and going. Carla's waiting and Kevlar helps us out and gives Carla a hug. I remember Carla. She smells of kitchen cooking and always has a snack for me. "Get in this house," she says. "Oh. Tiger, I have a surprise for you."

You do? I let her pat me. Pets are not allowed on the island, but an exception was made for the caretakers' foolish little dog, Birdy. And me. I scowl at Birdy. He remembers me from before and backs away. I don't even have to touch him. He might be twice my size, but a simple hiss or a snarl is enough to scare him off.

Kevlar gets our stuff. "We're traveling light." The duffle is theirs; the small suitcase has my things; toys, litter, box, food, and dishes.

"I'll show you to your room to freshen up, then I have lunch waiting in the kitchen."

Boston puts me on the floor in the giant entranceway which smells of wood polish like she used back home. It has dark wood paneling all around and is pleasantly cool. Hadn't noticed the warm outside until I felt the cool. Birdy keeps his distance.

Carla continues, "Fresh Dungeness crab salad."

My ears perk up. *Crab? Fresh crab? Is that my present?*

She leads us past a massive fireplace with benches and bookcases and we head upstairs. The first two doors are closed, and we stop at the third door down the hall. She opens it and motions us inside.

I sniff and walk in. Jump up on the bed and walk across it to the nightstand in front of the window. Settle there to watch the turkeys.

Cool.

"Come to the kitchen for lunch as soon as you freshen up," Carla says as she leaves.

Lunch. Yes. I stand, ready to go.

But Boston is exploring the closets and cupboards. Kevlar opens the suitcase, and he sets out my litter box and puts in some litter.

But I want to eat. Hurry. Hurry.

"Look, Kev," Boston says pulling the closet door wide open. "All built-in drawers and a full-length mirror on the inside of the door." She walks over to the bed.

"This quilt is hand made. All of it. Not a machine stitch in sight." She would know. She makes most of her own clothes. Not any of Kevlar's though. He is happy with store bought.

Seems to take them forever to wash up and I do use the litter box. Finally, I lead them down the staircase and follow voices to the kitchen. A huge room. The stove has, count them, four ovens. The sink looks like a trough. A large table in the center of the room is set with lunch. Boston puts my dishes down and I watch closely as Carla fills one with crab.

I saunter over. Breathe in and sigh. Crab. My very own dish of fresh crab. I notice Birdy gets kibble which he snarfs down while I'm still enjoying the bouquet of fresh crab. I settle in and don't pay too much attention to the conversation. It's typical stuff when old Park Service friends get together. Who retired. Who transferred. Who was promoted.

Boston tells them we are on our way to Reno for a seminar.

I get seconds and Birdie gets a milk bone he happily takes to his bed. After lunch we get a tour of the house. Carla gives us the history of the island in more detail than Pete had. Adds that the Carnegies, called Carn – e – geez, settled here and built homes. She points out the wood-work, the Tiffany chandeliers, the hand painted wallpaper, the round crystal doorknobs.

Yeah. Yeah. Yeah. Where are the mice?

The rooms are empty. She says, "Your room is one of the few with furniture. The Carnegies sent most every-thing to auction long ago when they sold the property to the Park Service." The house is boring, boring, boring. I check out each room. No mice or even droppings. Not even an old odor. Nothing to climb on or bat around or chase. I don't even find dust bunnies in the corners. Carla is a fastidious housekeeper.

Downstairs we pass another room with the door closed and she points at it and says, "We can go in here after dinner. It's the bill ards room."

Who is Bill Ards?

The tour doesn't take long because two whole wings are closed off. We finish in the basement. That's a room under the house; we don't have them in the Everglades.

Pete continues the narration. "This cellar has two rooms. The squash courts." He opens a door and shows us a large empty square room. Then leads us into the last room.

I take two steps inside and freeze.

Can't move. Not even my brain. Everything goes black. Dark all around. And then the recurrent nightmare of my drowning starts. I close my eyes but can still see the film unreel.

I take a breath. I can breathe. I'm not drowning. I try it again. Take a chance and open my eyes. I can see. And what I see is terrifying.

Water. A room full of water. In the cellar. A big lake of water.

Kevlar is watching me. I take another breath. Boston is busy with Carla. Kevlar walks over and picks me up. Holds me close. It helps. It helps a lot. I hang on tight. It was the shock of walking in on it. I'm not scared. I just like to know where it is. The water. It was the shock of it sneaking up on me that has me unsettled. I try another breath.

A swimming pool full of water in the cellar.

It doesn't smell like bay water or salt water. More like detergent. Who'd of thought? Who could have expected? How did it get here? Why?

Carla's voice filters in. Something about a swimming pool in the basement and how the pool helps cool the house.

Don't care.

Kevlar carries me out of the room and back to the safety of the squash courts where we wait for the others to finish looking, and then we head back to our room. He sets me gently on the bed with a pat, and they go off for their tour of Dungeness.

I take a long nap and wake up feeling better but bored and wander around the room; check the corners and under the bed. Find my toy and chase it around. It rolls into the closet because Boston left the door open. I catch it. Shake it and toss it and it falls down behind the duffle bag. I jump over the duffle and see something kind of yellow and flat sticking out from the under the bottom drawer. Paper. I worry it a bit. Tug on it with my incisors. Move it a tad. It's really wedged. I get a couple of claws into it and tug it most of the way out.

On old envelope. Nothing. I leave it still stuck and grab my toy and carry it to the bed.

There are voices out front and I jump to the nightstand

by the window to check. They're back. Carla is serving drinks on the front stoop which she calls the veranda, in an upper-class plummy voice. I sit and watch them and the turkeys out in the yard.

Why am I still upstairs all by myself? The turkeys are waiting.

I head downstairs, stop at the kitchen first to check the food dishes. Nothing except the dog food that even Birdy won't eat. I join everyone on the porch. Carla and Pete are in rocking chairs, and I decide against jumping on the glider with Kevlar and Boston. I want a closer look at the walking feathered turkeys. I step off the side of the porch and trot quickly across the crushed shell. The shell points hurt my pads, but I make it across to the soft grass.

Boston whispers hoarsely, "Tiger, get back here."

I twist one ear back at her and kind of crouch walk. When I get about ten feet away from the birds, I sink to my belly and scoot closer. Cool. It's easy. The turkeys don't even notice me, they are acorn-grabbing and insect-stabbing. And talking back and forth. In fact they have been chattering all the time I've been creeping up on them. They don't look like the turkey that comes out of the oven. Don't smell like it either. A sort of fight breaks out as two birds square off with their tail feathers spread. They are calling each other nasty names.

"Merow."

Oops. Didn't mean to say anything.

A movement catches my eye and I flinch. More creatures. Four legged. Smaller than the horses, but bigger than most dogs. My first thought is, how did a whole group? herd? of noisy large animals sneak up on me? My second is, they're naked. If they have fur, it's really fine. They all have wicked sharp hooves and some of them have tusks. Grunting and squealing, they dig in the ground. With their noses. Funny round flat noses. The ones with the tusks look dangerous. Two move closer. One black, one tan. They smell bad. Stare at me.

I creep backward.

Boston grabs me, hauls me up. "Tiger, those are boars, wild pigs. They're digging for acorns. But they can be dangerous."

No kidding. Those hooves or tusks could hurt a cat.

"You could say they are bacon, ham, or porkchops on the hoof."

Those are ham? And pork chops? Bacon? Where? How? This place is like an evil magic world.

She carries me back to the glider where I settle in her lap and try to figure out how I can get a porkchop.

When the sun sets, the mosquitoes come out and we go inside for dinner where Pete entertains us with stories about their time stationed in Everglades.

I'm more interested in my crab, served along with some fresh-caught redfish. Wonder when we get turkey and ham.

After dinner Pete suggests we retire to the bill ards room. And maybe *shoot some pool*. Hunh? The pool word makes me a little nervous. It's on the first floor, not in the cellar where the pool is, but I am cautious walking in and stop in the doorway to give it a long stare before entering. Dark wood paneling, large dark green leather chairs. A smoky smell. And a very large table toward the center of the room.

Pete walks over to the table and says, "I'll rack the balls."

Balls? Balls are fun. They roll and bounce. I jump up on the table for a better look. Lots of balls. All different colors. All collected together. I lunge for the one with the green stripe, but Kevlar catches me before I can touch it. Whisks me off the table.

Bummer. Not fair. He hands me off to Boston.

"Get a q stick," Pete says and both men get long sticks. We watch as Pete hits a white ball with his 'q stick'. The ball smashes into the other balls and they all scoot and roll across the table.

I could do that. Who needs a stick? This looks like fun. I wiggle to get down.

"Poor kitty," Boston says. "Always someone telling you no. Don't jump on the pigs. Don't chase the turkeys. Don't play with the pretty balls."

She hugs me, but I'm pretty frustrated. Not purring.

"I may have just the thing for him," Carla says and walks to a built-in cupboard which she opens and grabs a brown thing which she puts on the floor. Boston lets me down to investigate.

Just to be difficult, I sit. Glare.

Carla picks the thing up and sets it gently down in front of me. Birdy starts to come over, and I stop him with a glance, and since the thing is now in front of my paws I lean over to sniff.

Wow. Rabbit. Rabbit fur. I touch it and jump back when it squeaks, moves a tad. I give it a little push. It squeaks and jerks. Kind of jumps. I'm on it in a heartbeat, catching it in mid-roll.

"Did that thing just roll over by itself?" Boston asked. "What is it? Is it alive?"

"Rabbit covered plastic egg filled with jumping beans."

I don't care what it is, this thing is fun. I bat it across the room and chase after it. Who cares about those stupid colored balls, anyhow.

I wear myself out playing and am resting when the folks decide it's bedtime. I carry my bean toy upstairs with us and bring it to bed with me. To my spot on the foot of the bed and settle down to finish my nap.

What? What was that? Something. Not a noise, more like…well, a change in the air. I open my eyes. Kevlar is asleep and Boston is under the covers sitting up against the headboard with a book in her hand staring at the door. I look in that direction. There's a sort of thickness in the air. A little energy. The thickness has kind of a human shape in a long dress, but I can see through it. Can't really see it. Like when Boston puts an ice cube in my water dish, the cube seems to blend in, disappear. The shape is like that. It seems to come through the doorway. Bringing a ripple of cold. And a kind of pressure. It moves, glides? floats? toward the nightstand.

Boston half chokes.

My fur stands on end.

It reaches the nightstand.

The light goes out.

The figure shimmers in the darkness.

It moves over toward Boston.

I don't get a sense of good or bad. More like curiosity. But I jump up and move between her and the shape. Dig in my toes. Arch my back. Stick my tail straight up. My fur raises. Sticks all the way out.

"*GRRR!*." I snarl. Warn it off.

It hesitates. Stops. Then moves slowly to the door. Out. The door closes.

Well. What was that? This is the weirdest place.

Boston takes a deep breath. Pokes Kevlar. Pokes him again, harder. "Up. Up."

"Wanh?" he mumbles.

"G.. gh… g…," she stutters.

"What?" Kevlar says more distinctly.

She tries again. "G… g… ghost."

He reaches over and turns on the light by his side of the bed.

"What?"

"A ghost. A ghost just came in and turned off my light."

He frowns. Looks around. "You fell asleep reading and had a bad dream."

"No." She spits that out. "No. I was awake reading. It

came in and turned off the light. Why would the light be out if I had fallen asleep reading?"

That stops him a second.

She said, "Tiger saw it."

He looks at me doubtfully. He asks, "Why is his fur sticking up all over? Why is it so cold in here?"

"The ghost brought in the cold."

He takes a long look at her. At me. My fur is still all sticking out, and my back is arched. I try to tone it down a little.

"The ghost scared him," she says.

Did not.

"You're shivering. Get over here." He drags her close to him, puts his arms around her. He rubs her. "You're freezing."

No one is comforting me.

Her teeth are chattering. "Yes. The ghost was cold."

He keeps rubbing her back, her arms.

Well maybe I don't want to be comforted. Don't like it when people rub my fur back and forth.

He pulls the blanket around her shoulders. "Tell me what happened."

She takes a deep breath. "A ghost came in and turned off the light." She sounds annoyed with the repetition.

"No. Tell me what you saw. Details."

Calmer now. She tells him about the shape and the cold. About me jumping up. She wraps her arms around herself. "I'm freezing."

"You are." He holds her tight. "Seems to me the cat

protected you. Jumped between you and the ghost." He laughs at that and shakes his head.

I prance over and nudge him under the chin.

"Good cat," he says and gives me a pat, helping my fur lay flat.

"You warming up?" he asks Boston. "Can I leave you a minute? Check the hall. See if it left any sign? Wasn't Pete, was it?"

She shakes her head back and forth. "It wasn't anybody. I could see right through it, like you can see through ice. God, I'm exhausted," She rubs her arms again. "Should we tell Pete his house is haunted?"

"Not tonight. In the morning." He gets out of bed, opens the door, walks into the hall.

I watch closely.

Comes back, closes the door, and gets into bed and turns off his light.

I sneak under the covers with them. No one complains.

In the morning they have another discussion about the ghost. Did they both dream it? No. We go down to break-fast. Eggs and bacon and ham this morning. Wild pig? I get some of everything. Birdy gets his kibble and a milk bone.

"I saw a ghost last night," Boston says after Kevlar motions her with his chin.

Carla stiffens; a slice of bacon halfway to her mouth and looks quickly at Pete. Guiltily?

I watch the bacon.

Can almost feel the air chill, but not as cold as last night.

No one laughs at Boston. Carla has her tongue between her teeth. Pete looks uneasy. Says, "Dungeness is the haunted house. At least that's the tale. I don't think anyone still living claims to have seen the ghosts. None have ever been reported here at Plum Orchard."

Kevlar gives him a searching look. "Reported? What does that mean?"

Pete looks uncomfortable.

Carla speaks up. "You tell them Pete. Or I will. These are our friends."

His shoulders slump. He looks down and speaks slowly. "The ghost, for want of a better term. She's unnerving. Not malevolent. Just walks the halls at night. Turns out lights, closes doors. Leaves behind a cold chill in the rooms. A family member, we think. Carla and I."

"That's what happened. Exactly what happened last night," Boston says. "She came in and turned off my light. Closed the door on her way out. It was freezing."

Pete and Carla nod agreement. "That's the reason we live down here in the maids quarters. She doesn't come down here. We've done some research but can't find anything that matches. No ghost is documented. We haven't told anyone. No one would believe us. In fact, they might decide to move us out of our caretaker position if they thought we were seeing ghosts."

Boston says, "I'll tell you. Even after last night. I still don't believe in ghosts. I saw her, felt the cold. Saw the light go out. Saw Tiger see her. Nevertheless, part of me wants to say, dream. Even though it was still cold when I woke Kevlar and Tiger's fur was all spiked. The ghost, her whole appearance is clear in my mind. I can shut my eyes and still see that, that thing, apparition." Boston shudders.

Kevlar says, "I almost wish we could stay tonight. Trap the thing. Get a picture."

Is he crazy?

Pete is shaking his head. "She appears sporadically. No schedule. We slept up there and put up with it for eight months. And I did take pictures. Nothing shows up. Empty space." He shrugs. "She might return tonight. Or not for a month."

There is silence around the table. Carla eats her bacon absently.

Darn.

"How does Birdy react to the ghost," Kevlar asks.

"Hides under the covers. Brave dog. Not. But can't blame him; wanted to do the same thing myself," Pete says as he gives the dog a fond glance.

They laugh.

Boston says, "You should at least give her a name."

"We have. Matilda."

"Matilda," Boston repeats. "Good name for a ghost. Do you know why she walks?"

I tilt my head and stare at her. *I heard the ghost tell you. Didn't you hear?*

Both Pete and Carla shake their heads. "I don't think we'll ever know."

"Oh, well. I'll help you clean up, Carla, and then I have to pack. Mostly Tiger's gear. I have that seminar later and we don't want to miss the ferry because of Matilda."

Pete goes to get the electric cart and I check my food dish again. Maybe I missed some bacon, but even the smell is licked off.

Back in the room Boston reaches in the closet and tells Kevlar, "Carla said to leave the bed. She'll strip it later."

I notice my paper toy hung under the drawer and claw it out some more.

"Okay. I'll clean his litter and pack up his stuff. Too bad we can't stay longer."

"You didn't really want to stay and hunt the ghost, did you?" she asks.

"What?" He frowns. "No. I meant just to visit." He snorts. "Not to hunt a ghost. We could spend a month waiting for it to come back. And then what? No. Like you, I don't believe in ghosts. If I'm going to hunt something it will be solid." And he grabs her and kisses her.

I like to see them together, but it makes me a little jealous. That I have to share her. He reaches around her into the closet for the duffle and drags it out. Then gets my suitcase.

"Huh? What's that?" he bends down and grabs my paper.

Hey. That's mine.

He gives it a hefty tug and pulls it free.

"You lose an envelope, honey?" he asks.

"Not mine. Let's see."

Kevlar hands it over.

"Has claw marks on it. And some tooth punctures.

Tiger must have pulled it out from under the drawer. Wow. This is old." She opens the flap. Looks inside.

"Money."

She shows him. "Gold certificates. Ten-dollar bills. Five of them. All dated 1928."

Kevlar takes one. "Can't trade those in for gold anymore. Probably only has collector's value. We can check these bills on-line. On your cell."

He steps to the door and calls Pete.

He and Carla come in and Kevlar explains, handing them the envelope.

All this fuss over paper? Not even scrunched up rattling paper you can play with.

Pete takes the bills out of the envelope and lays them on the bed.

Boston reads from her cell, "Value to collectors only. Depends on grade. 1928 Right?"

"Yeah," Pete replies.

She does some more things with her cell. "Tens that year are very common. Ours look brand new though and uncirculated."

"Doesn't really matter," Pete says. "They belong to the Park Service. They definitely have some historical value. Yeah. Take some pictures with your cell, Boston, and email them to me. I'll forward them to my supervisor."

"Wait there's another piece of paper in here," Kevlar says. Pulls it out and unfolds it. Reads out loud, 'Darling, Pack your things. Meet me at the gazebo in the garden when the lights are all out. We'll go to town and get married and come back tomorrow. I love you.' No signature."

"Wow," Carla breathes. "An assignation. In the garden. After dark. How romantic."

Becca says, "The ghost. That's what she was doing. Turning out the lights. So, she could go meet him."

That's what I heard the ghost say. 'I have to turn out the lights and meet Roger.'

"But the money is here. And the note. They ran away together but were planning to come back. Something happened."

Carla holds up her hand. "Wait. I remember a story about one of the Carnegie nieces. Running off with a sailer."

"But the money is still here. Why. And if she's a ghost, that means she's dead." Boston stops. Pulls her hair. "Well, of course she's dead it's been nearly a hundred years. But I mean she must have died around the time she was turning off the lights. Or she wouldn't be walking?"

She growls. Actually growls. Throws her hands up in the air. "I don't care. I don't want to know. I don't even believe in ghosts."

But then she walks over to Carla and whispers, "Yes. I do want to know, if you find out what happened."

I walk over to look at the gold certificates. Green with a gold circle. They don't smell moldy. Just old. I reach out to touch, but Kevlar grabs me up. "Oh, no you don't"

And he stuffs me in the cage. "Time to go, Tiger."

I turn around to spit out something nasty, but he leans

down and says, "We have to go back to the mainland, and you have to be in the box for the ride over on the ferry. Rules. You knew this was coming. It's to protect you, to keep you safe, out of harm's way. It's not a jail cell. It's more of a second home. A mobile home, without the wheels. We can call it something else. A cat cave. Armored car. Fort. Bullet proof tank. We don't want you hurt."

Maybe.

"You can sit with us. On the bench. We'll be the only ones on the boat. The wind can blow through your fur." He reaches into his pocket, pulls out my jumping bean toy, and puts it in my armored car with me.

Okay. Truce. But still, I give him a just wait stare, the tip of my tongue sticking out my lips.

SHAKES, SHIVERS, AND JACKPOTS

We're in San Francisco, visiting Thad and Erin on our way to Reno. I wasn't listening when Boston told me why. Or who they were.

Thad stares disapprovingly at me. Erin frowns. "You said you would have a cat. It's kind of big. Are you sure it's not a dog?"

They think I'm a dog? Me? A dog? They think I'm a dog? Really? Humph. They look right at me and ask, "Are you sure that's a cat." Really? I am large for a cat, bigger than some stupid yapper dogs. I'm a Maine Coon cat. So, I don't have the tufted ears, but I have the weight. They should show some respect. A dog?

It???

And then Erin says, "Doesn't cat fur makes people itchy? And cats can have fleas."

My fur can make people itchy? I might have fleas? And

a dog doesn't have fur? Or fleas? I ask you. How could anyone be so silly.

I hate this place.

"We can't stay long," Kevlar tells Thad and Erin, "We could leave him in the car," he says doubtfully. Even reluctantly.

What? How can you say that? How dare you. Leave me in the car?

But they turn him down. Even say I don't have to stay in the cat carrier.

Boston whispers to me when she opens the carrier door, "You are lucky you don't have to stay in the car. Do not jump on shelves. Or the table."

Not that I would. Nothing interesting up there. Argh.

Thad and Erin watch me like they've never seen a cat before, as if I might turn into a ferocious wolf and attack them and tear them limb from limb. Actually, I think they may be a little afraid. Well. Okay. That might be good.

"He's kind of fat isn't he" Thad asks.

"He's a Maine Coon cat. They come big." Kevlar defends me. I might not be Kevlar's favorite person, but he doesn't like them saying I look fat. FAT. Kevlar can call me fat but not these folks.

"What kind of kibble does he eat?"

Kibble? They think I eat kibble. I ask you. Kibble. No chicken, no beef. No ham. Not even cheese. Kibble. Who are they to say what I should be eating? Ugh.

Kevlar says quickly, "We need to be in Reno and can't stay but a little while." He made that up.

Boston breathes a sigh of relief. Thad and Erin too.

Me most of all. I sit quietly and they seem to forget I'm here. So I sneak off and explore. And listen.

I hate this place. Hate it. Boooring. No rats, no birds, nothing to watch or chase or pounce on.

Erin announces happy hour. A time for cocktails. Not bird tails, or cat tails or even peacock tails. Humans have strange names for things which often make no sense. And the happy hour isn't an hour either, but happy hour means you drink cocktails and get happy. Cocktails have alcohol.

Alcohol burns my nose when I sniff it. Yuk.

Boston says alcohol does to people what catnip does to cats. Erin's already a little tipsy. Happy hour began early, before we got here, and looks to last the rest of the night.

Boston is sticking to water. Kevlar has been nursing one beer. He has to drive.

I hate it here. I am bored, bored, bored. Really bored. Nothing to hunt. Nothing to chase. No food dish to check. Bummer that one. Not even anything to knock off a shelf. Except, maybe, those fluffy yellow feathers. Way up at the very back of the shelf of the wall unit, excuse me, etagere. Our hostess corrected Boston when she called it an exquisite rattan bookcase.

Like the meaningless word cocktails, they can't just call it a bookshelf or knickknack shelf. It's an etagere. Doesn't matter to me what they call it. No one is watching me, so I decide to check out the feathers and I slip away. I can reach the yellow feathers from the top of the little corner table. Pretty sure.

It's an easy jump to the tabletop. But the table is rickety and wobbles for a few seconds. The top is littered with knickknacks near the wall. Hidden from a cat on the floor.

I raise up on my haunches and snag a feather with my claws snatching it out of the vase.

Oops. They all escape. Float down.

Hey cool. I jump after them and strike out to bat one around as it floats to the floor. But it moves even before I touch it. They all do, buffeted by the draft.

Way cool. I chase them around without even touching them.

"Tiger. No."

Boston's stern voice. In a loud whisper.

I stop and put on my innocent disguise. *Me? I didn't do anything. Just sitting here and these feathers floated in front of me.*

The floor trembles. Shakes. Hunh? I dig my claws in. Try to. But the floor is tile, and I can't get a grip. I start to hunker down and the floor tilts. Tilts! The floor! I slide a few inches, claws screeching. Kevlar is braced in the doorway, feet flat on the floor, knees slightly bent, hands pushing on the doorframe. Thad is gently rocking, swaying, like a palm frond in the breeze.

Help. Boston. She's stuck on the sofa, her knees higher than her waist, her feet in the air. She tries to lean forward, struggles to stand. The feathers float up in the air and around.

But I can't move to catch them.

Help. At least I'm sliding in Boston's direction.

The whole house shakes.

Erin picks up her soda, well cocktail, her fourth, if anyone is counting, and takes a sip, legs slightly braced.

Boston manages to reach down and grab me before I careen past the sofa, and she pulls me close into her. Everything is shaking. The couch rocks, side to side. The hanging light, chandelier it's called, swings back and forth.

The walls grumble. A book jumps off the shelf and slams to the floor.

I dig in and Boston hollers and grabs my front paws, gently pulling my claws out of her arm. "Hey," she admonishes me.

Oh. Sorry. I didn't mean to do that.

Erin walks over and picks the book up and places it back on the swaying shelf.

The picture frames rattle against the wall. The knick-knacks knock together on the shelf.

Boston is still trying to stand, but all her weight is settled in the back corner of the couch.

Houses are not supposed to shake and move. I bare my teeth.

"Grrrr." I can't help it, the growl comes out.

The rattling stops, just as suddenly as it started.

I take a breath but am still ready to run and hide. Don't know where or how. Just run. Boston tightens her grip on me. "It's okay," she says soothingly. "It's okay."

I am not sure she believes it.

The light slows in its swing.

"Well," Kevlar says, not quite steady, "Been a long time since I've been in an earthquake. Have to thank you folks for arranging it. Don't think Boston has ever experienced one."

Earth quake? It sure did.

Boston says, "No. No. Can't say as I have. Though I knew immediately what it was. No mistaking it. Appreciate the opportunity. I'm a geologist, and an earthquake has always been on my to-do list."

Huh? Not me. I didn't need that. If I want the world to shake, I can climb a coconut tree and get out on a palm frond.

"There will probably be aftershocks," Erin says hopefully. Even gleefully.

I sigh. *I hate this place.*

"I'm sure," Boston says looking around. For a place to run and hide? Like me?

Erin says, "I need to refresh our cocktails," and goes for more drinks.

But Boston says, "We really have to be going, we want to get to our motel before dark, and it's snowing pretty hard where we are headed." She starts to collect our things.

And we are not going to tell anyone about the feathers?

In a few minutes we're on our way and I get to sit up front in Boston's lap. Kevlar is driving, Boston navigating and talking.

"Well, an earthquake. Thank you, Kev. I knew right away what that was and intended to jump up and run out the door and down the street screaming. But I couldn't get off the couch. The couch saved me from making an idiot of myself."

Really?

She continues. "And I had wondered why her knick-knacks were all lined up at the back of the shelves. Now I understand. Too bad the feathers sailed out. I wonder if that happens often."

Kevlar looks at her. "Only when a bad cat is visiting probably."

We both look at him.

"I hadn't thought anyone saw him do that. All in all though, to tell you the truth, I prefer our hurricanes. They come with a warning and give you time to prepare." She took a breath, "But I'd like to suggest next time we visit; we skip this stop."

Next time? No. No next time. I am done traveling.

Kevlar agrees. "It was uncomfortable. Had to visit though. She's an old friend of my aunt's. And the earthquake was a fitting end."

It is snowing real hard and I help drive, but I can't see out the window. The wind is blowing snow across the windshield.

The car goes into a skid. A bit like an earthquake.

Home, take me home.

Kevlar gets us back on track. A few minutes later we go into another skid which Kevlar corrects. He's holding tightly to the wheel, steering, pumping the brakes.

"How far to that motel?" he asks between gritted teeth.

"One mile the sign said. It's right up the road. I made reservations online. Donner Pass Inn."

"You're kidding."

"No. One mile."

"I mean about the Donner Pass Inn. We are seriously staying in a motel in Donner Pass? In a snowstorm? That is just perfect. First a few hours with a couple who don't know about cats or dogs, an earthquake, and now we get to spend a snowbound winter night in Donner Pass. Just perfect.

"Why? What? How come?" Boston asks.

That's a lot of questions.

"You don't know that story? About Donner Pass?"

"No, and now I'm not sure I want to know."

"Nutshell. The Donner wagon train became snowbound here. The settlers ate each other."

"Oh gross."

Settlers? People? People ate people?

He glances at her sideways. "There's the turnoff. Hope we survive the night." He chuckles, sort of, and turns down a road covered in snow and parks in front of a large mountain cabin.

"No lights outside," Boston says nervously.

"Emergency lights on the eaves. Must have lost power. I'll check. You two wait here."

I watch him climb the steps, on a shovel wide path. Just as he reaches for the door it swings open and a jolly round man greets him. They talk a few minutes, and he comes back.

"They have our reservation. Some of the townsfolk are here. There's no power in the pass. He says bring the kitty." Kevlar laughs.

Kitty? The jolly guy called me a kitty? Doesn't he recognize a Maine Coon cat when he sees one?

It is really cold. And still is when we step through the door into a small entranceway. The tips of my ears feel almost frozen. The jolly man pulls the inside door open for us and motions us through. Warm air flows out.

He peeks in at me in my cage as we pass. "Nice kitty," he says, and I glare at him.

Kitty?

He stoops lower. "That cat is huge. What is he, a bobcat?"

I soften my glare.

Kevlar responds, "Well fed."

Switch my glare to Kevlar.

"Go inside, we have a fire going."

Fire? He has a fire going? Why? Where? I look toward Boston, but she doesn't appear concerned as she carries me in.

"I'll secure these doors. Was just locking up for the night. Family style supper, still on the table, help yourselves." He laughs and ushers us into a huge warm and toasty room.

It's wonderful. Dim and dark. Lots of places to explore, hunt. The fire is in a large, bricked hole in the wall. A fireplace. This one covers a full wall and is big enough for a man to walk into it. There is a grill over the fire with pots on it.

Wonderful smells.

Three guys are grouped together in the center of the room playing musical instruments and singing. They do that in Flamingo, too.

"Sit down, let the cat free. He can roam. The doors are closed to keep the heat in, and no one will let him out. You'll find dishes by the fire, pot roast, venison stew, corn, um, mashed potatoes, unless Chad, over there with the guitar, ate it all, gravy,

Maybe someone will tell me what ven-i-sin is.

"Get some for your cat, too."

I think I like this man. Sure smells good.

Then he adds, "By the looks of him he probably needs some food."

Nasty.

Boston bends down to let me out. "Don't leave the room," she says.

Not happening until I eat. And I want to explore too. Musty smells coming from the corners. Smells like a barn. Old smell of horses. Maybe cows. And fresh mouse scents. Animal skins on the walls. Animal heads too. Things with big horns. Makes my skin itch. At least I don't see any cats on the wall. I shiver at the thought. Boston will protect me.

"Food first, as soon as we get our coats off then you can explore after we eat," she tells me. But I have time to make a full circuit of the room while she fills plates. Find a mouse hole with a family of the creatures inside. I can smell five. No six. But the entrance is too small for me to get a paw into.

I head over to remind her it's dinner time when that man with the guitar, Chad, calls, "Here kitty, here kitty."

I don't even hear him.

"Want some chicken?" he asks holding out a big piece of meat, swinging it back and forth.

Ooops. Well, maybe I can hear a faint voice. I move a few steps in his direction.

"Can your cat eat chicken?"

"No bones," Boston says coming to look. She nods to both of us, and I step closer. He puts the meat on the floor.

I sniff it. Sniff him too. He has a nice woodsy smell. I pick up the piece delicately and back up a few steps.

They do the human introduction thing, shake hands and exchange names. "Chad," he calls himself. The guy who might have eaten all the mashed potatoes.

"Don't try to pat him," Boston says. "He's not really friendly. Maybe after you have fed him a few pieces he might let you touch him."

So, I can be bribed. I chew on the chicken. Juicy.

He puts down a piece of beef for me. I am going to like this, Chad. He has a beard all over his chin and down on his chest. Weird.

I finish his meat and go check my food dish and clean it all up.

They stop playing and everyone listens as Chad tells a story.

And someone puts more food in my dish. Meat bits cooked in butter. Red in the middle, seared brown on the outside. Yummy. Roasted turkey too. I miss the beginning of the story.

Chad is chanting. "The wagon train was snowed in. They sent out an explorer to try to find help or a way out. But the snow was too deep. They were stuck. Four months. Trapped in the pass. They ran out of food."

Oh oh. I look up. Ran out of food?

"They ate the horses."

Yuck.

"The oxen."

Double yuck.

"The family pets."

What? I'm so shocked I stop chewing. *How could they? Does that mean they ate the cats? Or just the dogs? Maybe a few birds.*

But no. They couldn't eat cats because they wouldn't be able to catch them. Kevlar hadn't said anything about pets.

"And then," Chad lowers his voice and with a wicked twist to his words says, "They ate each other. They resorted to cannibalism."

People ate people? Gulp. I had thought Kevlar was kidding about people eating people.

Chad continues, "But there is more to the story. New information. Preston and Child have written about it. "Not all the settlers who were eaten were human. Nor all those who survived."

He hits the drum. "Baboom."

What?

"Wolves," Chad says. Soft with a hint of danger.

Wolves? Wolves ate people?

"Not Donner Pass wolves," he cautions. "But werewolves."

Boston laughs.

I know what wolves are. We saw them in Yellow Stone Park.

Wear wolves? What does that mean?

Chad continues his story in a spooky low voice. "Werewolves and cannibals ate people and other werewolves. Forty-eight pioneers survived. Today some deny any cannibalism. People would rather be thought of as non-human monster werewolves then as cannibals. Werewolves may walk among us today."

He winks at us. "The story ends. Maybe. It's bedtime for me."

The group breaks up. Everyone is staying here tonight. *Do we have to worry? Will they eat us? All three of us? Not just the family pet?*

No. There is still plenty of food on the table.

Boston helps me into my carrying case and we head back out into the cold and walk to our cabin, which is almost as cold inside as outside.

"Werewolves," Boston snorts.

"There are two books out now describing Donner Pass cannibals and werewolves," Kevlar tells her.

"Werewolves don't exist. They're legends."

"Who is to say? There must be some basis in reality."

"You don't even believe that," Boston says and then informs him. "Most legends do have a basis in reality. The werewolf legend probably started when some wild dog or wolf grabbed a child. And someone says he saw a human change into a wolf under a full moon. A werewolf."

Kevlar dips his head. "Human prey."

"If you say you believe there are werewolves, I'm going to have to say that Tiger is a werecat, and you better not sleep tonight."

I am? What's a wear cat?

He gives me a quick panicked glance, then laughs and grabs her for a kiss. "If he were, he would have eaten me a long time ago. I'm not worried."

Boston checks her tablet. "Hey look. There really are werecats. As found on Google. Called lykol. Lykols are a natural domestic shorthair cat. Except they look kind of fake. Look just like how some people think a werecat would look if they existed." She shows Kevlar a photo.

I catch a glimpse. Talk about mangy. *Ugly.*

She puts down her tablet and they crawl into bed with their clothes on, and I decide to sleep under the covers with them. Share my body heat and protect them. Against werewolves.

Stupid stories. I curl up against Boston's belly. Kevlar is spooned behind her, his arm around her waist. It's dark and toasty here under the covers. Comfy. I keep my ears open for wolves. And drift off to sleep.

Panting. Loud panting.

Werewolves. Werewolves and werecats. Surrounding the bed. Growling. Tongues hanging out. Spittle flying from their lips. Eyes and fangs glowing in the firelight.

No smell. No stink.

One giant wolf moves closer. Reaches out. A paw? A hand?

I shrink backward but hit a soft barrier.

Pressure near my paw and I pull it back. Struggle to raise my head but another soft barrier is holding me down. I try to shake free.

A werecat comes for me. Its fangs shining and silver. Its fur tinged with silver in the black night.

I struggle to drag myself up. But a sudden pressure on my chest, forces me down

Can't move. Can't breathe.

"Merow."

"Stop," Boston says.

I'm grabbed around the middle.

The werecat. It's got me. I can't move.

"Roowwwll!!" I scream. *Werewolves! Werecats! They are attacking! Run!*

"Tiger stop," Boston says firmly. "Tiger," she orders in a stern voice. "Settle down. Stop."

What? Boston? And suddenly I'm awake. Trapped under her arm. Shake my head so my mouth and nose are free of the blanket. Take a deep breath.

Her hand lifts from holding me down and strokes my middle. Gently.

I look around. No werewolves. No werecats. Just us. "You're keeping us awake. Settle down."

Ohhh. A bad dream?

I take another deep breath.

She strokes me again. "Sleep."

Can't. Still see the werecat.

Kevlar murmurs, "Easy. Both of you. It's okay. Sleep." And he strokes down Boston's arm, lays his hand over hers, his fingertips curling around my tummy, protecting me from nightmare cats and wolves.

I sigh, close my eyes.

Wake to a clear and crisp morning dawn.

After a hearty breakfast we head to Reno. It's a ride through trees and mountains. Not flat like the Everglades. We are staying in a hotel kaseeno. We enter a huge room full of noise, constant and unending. Flashing, dazzling lights. Incessant movement. People in a hurry, dressed in loud colors, radiating energy and despair.

We don't stay in that room long but head for the l-or-vator. I hate them.

My stomach suddenly goes down and the rest of me goes up as the l-or-vator goes up.

"Yawl."

"It's ok Tiger." Boston says gently.

Is not.

The vator door opens onto a long corridor where the lighting and noise are a little dimmer. We walk to a door and Kevlar puts a keycard in a slot and opens it. We'll be here one day, or I will be. I will stay in our room. Alone. Boston will spend the day at her meeting. And Kevlar is going to gambol. I don't think that's like running and jumping playfully in the woods.

I get a full food dish.

Oh, yeah. Okay.

It isn't actually quiet in the room. Hints of bells and loud music seep through the walls and floor along with energy and desperation. An edgy nervousness. There is also the smell of stale cigarette smoke and chemicals. It turns out to be a very long day for me, broken up at frequent intervals when Kevlar comes to check on me and refill my dish.

I nap in between visits. Earthquakes and snowstorms and werewolves have me worn out.

When Boston comes back from her seminar, she and Kevlar both go to gambol. We go to bed late. Get up early and, finally, head for the airport and home. To my very own bed. My toys. I miss my refrigerator and my stove.

We wait in a quiet, almost peaceful corner at the airport for our plane. We'll be seated in the front row again, and I might be able to walk some in front of our seats, on the leash. But I am warned not to intimidate the service dog like I did on the plane ride here.

Bummer. Well, is it my fault the stupid dog was a wimp, like Birdy. I just sort of hissed at him, and he lay down with his nose in his tail.

Boston is holding me, rocking me like a baby, half up on her shoulder. And pacing. "Soon, now," she whispers. Kevlar is playing 'the slot' or one-armed bandit. I don't see any arms. Or bandits. Who knows? He plugs a twenty-dollar bill into 'the slot' and pushes some buttons on the keyboard, slaps at the screen where pictures are whirling around. Kind of like the Whirling Dervish. The pictures stop.

He does it again. Trying to slap the red balls.

I could slap a couple of those. Better than him. Hey, that might be kind of fun. I surprise Boston, push off out of her arms, and jump down onto the keyboard. Bounce a few steps and slap at the rolling screen. Bounce the other way.

Yes.

Kevlar grabs me across the chest and lifts me off the keyboard just as the slot explodes. Goes crazy.

Fireworks. Sirens blaring. Whistles blowing. Lights flashing all over, And something clattering deep in the machine. Echoing through the room.

Oops. Didn't do nothing. Wasn't me. The machine just went crazy. I didn't break it.

People come rushing toward us. Kevlar hands me to Boston who holds me tight while jumping up and down. Like the red balls.

She exclaims, "Good cat. Smart cat. You won a giant jackpot."

Hah? I did? Won a jack pot. We got a pot named jack?

I look around. The people are all smiling and clapping.

Because I won the pot?

Okay. Maine Coon cats are really smart.

Kevlar says, "Tuna and shrimp. He gets tuna and shrimp from now on."

Alright. And we get to go home. With the pot.

REDWINGS

I am the stealthy stalker. The Maine Coon cat hunter. I leap and land on the bird, exactly as planned, my front feet curled around him.

I lift one toe to check on my catch. What? Flattened grass and a twig, firmly clutched under my front paws? Not a little bird. How did this happen? Where did he go?

Maybe he slipped out between my toes. But how? It was a perfect attack. Perfect. I stalked the stupid bird for ten minutes while it hopped all around totally unaware of me.

I look around, but I don't see him.

"Argh."

Not my fault. He just vanished. Stupid bird. I should be stripping off his feathers now.

Yuk. Have never actually done that. But I could. Pull out feathers. Or maybe I should get my Lady to pull the feathers. That sounds smarter. Except she probably wouldn't be happy if I caught a bird. Maybe it's a good thing the stupid bird disappeared.

Oh well. Darn.

Ooh.

I freeze.

I hope no one saw. Move my eyes to check in front. No one watching. Twist my ears around back. Listen. Nothing. Lick a spot high on my chest to test movement behind me.

Nothing there. Lick another spot.

Something there.

Squirrel. Yoda. He's okay. He's a Mangrove Fox squirrel, Boston says, with a little admiration in her voice. He is big for a squirrel like I am for a cat. He has this black head and grayish white nose and ears. Golden brown underneath and darker on top. Big fluffy tail with a white tip.

He has part of a pond apple in his mouth. The apples are green, about the size of an egg. Leathery outside with lots of winged seeds inside. He likes those. I've seen him eat the coco plums too and they are mostly a big seed with a thin layer of flesh. No accounting for taste.

Did he see? If he did, he doesn't smirk. Once I saw him go after a lubber grasshopper. Missed it. Kind of like my little bird. He seems to look at me with sympathy. We respect each other.

He kind of shrugs and walks over to the seagrape where he lives and climbs up.

I'm done hunting, I'm tired, so I curl up on a sunny spot on the pavement and go to sleep. And dream I'm eating bacon.

"CLICK. CLICK. CHAC, CLICK, CLICK. CLICK."

Sigh.

"CLICK. CHAC. CHAC"

Bacon goes poof. Not asleep anymore. Who could sleep with all this clicking and chacking noise? All around me. Everywhere.

I open one eye, a sliver width, both inner and outer lid. Directly in front of me, a red-winged blackbird. The bright red orange yellow shoulder patch on both glossy black wings identifies him. And he is pecking on the pavement. "CLICK, CLICK."

In. Front. Of. My. Nose. In Front Of My Nose. Must be a dream. I shut the eye. See an afterimage of the bird on the inside of the lid. No sane bird would be pecking the pavement inches away from a Maine Coon cat's mouth. Not unless it is suicidal.

Deep breath. Dreaming. Must be.

I take another peek. Squint through both lids. The stupid bird is still there. And not alone. Two of them. No, wait. Three. I open both eyes. A whole herd of red-winged.

I close my eyes. Tight.

Not a dream. I can hear them all around me. Not loud. But constant. Pecking on the pavement. "Peck, click, click. Peck. Peck".

Open my eyes. They are in a circle all around me, like a halo. Dozens of them. I'm beginning to feel a little threatened. I may have to defend myself. Stupid birds. I flatten my eyes.

"Conk-la-reeeee. Conk-la-reee."

Singing now.

"Chak, chac, chac. Chit chit chit." Stupid red-winged.

Nap time is over. Sigh.

It must be close to mealtime.

Ha. Ha. Mealtime? Dinner is right in front of me. I swivel my head slowly to the right. Slowly to the left.

My jaw drops down. "Cackle."

Oops. I didn't mean to do that. A cackle is a sure sign of need. I never cackle. A Coon cat never cackles. We just go out and get what we want. We don't cackle at something we want. We grab it. And I'm gonna pounce on this nice juicy redwing.

"Caaackle."

Oh, no. My mouth cackled again. A long one.

I hope no one heard.

The stupid birds don't hear it. They're just pecking away. I narrow my eyes again. I select one. An especially fat one. A bright colored one. Stupid bird. Not that I'd eat it. I mean those feathers might get stuck in my mouth if no one pulled them off for me.

But I can slap it.

I ease over onto my belly. Paws on the ground.

"What the heck is going on out here?" Kevlar asks in a loud voice. "Why is there a flock of birds surrounding Tiger?"

Kevlar? I sure hope he didn't hear me cackle.

Is he laughing? It sure sounds like he might be laughing. I squint up at him.

He's looking directly at me. And he is. He is laughing at me. And it's his fault. This is all his fault. The birds have forgotten how dangerous I am because he took me away on vacation. I give Kevlar my best flat eyed, ears all the way back, glare.

I'm going to get him.

He chuckles. "Looks like your cat has some new buddies Boston. How does he get them to stay so close?"

Boston is here too? Of course, she is. I always bring her out with me. I turn my head all the way back. Slowly. I don't want to scare the birds. I'm still hoping to capture one.

She's snapping pictures? Why is she taking pictures? Of the red-winged? Me?

This is turning into a bad nightmare.

She says, "I spilled a bag of shelled pumpkin seeds. And Tiger decided to take a nap on that spot."

Didn't know those seeds were here now did I?

She continues, "I didn't have the heart to disturb him after he fell asleep. And then the birds came."

I look at the stupid birds again. My lower jaw drops open and I feel another cackle coming. I can't stop it. "C*a ca cah.*"

Geez, now I sound like the stupid birds.

I jump up mid-cackle and three birds skitter away just out of reach. The rest of the flock just kind of flows backward a few inches, like they're riding a wave.

I stand, take a quick step, and whomp at the stupid bird closest to me. Try to. He slips beyond my reach, buffeted by the wind from my swipe. Doesn't even notice me. Stupid bird.

My mouth opens in a snarl, my upper lip pulls back, my eye teeth hanging out.

I charge right into the midst of them.

They just float away gently to both sides.

I think I hear Kevlar laughing. Bob and Wolf are out now too, watching. Wolf with a sly grin. Stupid cat.

I walk stiff legged through the flock and it separates around me giving me a path.

Finally, I'm outside their circle and stalk over to Kevlar's truck and claw his tire. I attack it. Tear at it. Scratch it. Stab it. Dig at it. Bite it hard.

Take that, you stupid bird.

And now my mouth hurts.

Sluggo comes out with a click of his claws and the tinkle of his dog tags. Jackson comes with him.

What? Is everyone coming to see me humiliated? Well, Maine Coon cats don't do humiliation. We move on. I wasn't cackling. I was warning those stupid birds to keep their distance. And they did. That sort of halo thing they had going around me.

Sluggo sees the birds and charges through the midst of the flock, scattering them in all directions.

Sure. The stupid birds notice him.

He charges a few more times. Back. Forth. Races through them. They are gone now. He turns around and sees me. Prances over, pleased with himself. A big grin on his face, his silly tongue hanging out. Gives me a wet lick up the side of my face.

Ugh.

Stupid dog.

I snarl at him, just for effect. But he simply grins and then rushes off to charge the empty spot again. Then he goes to each person and wiggles for a pat and soft word.

But the silly dog worked some sort of magic. Most of my anger and frustration are gone. I consider my next move. Sluggo is sniffing out spots to pee. He finds two and uses them. Wolf and I both watch him in amazement.

Now he's searching out a third? He's such a dog.

Boston calls Bob and Kevlar over to look at her pictures and they gather around her. Kind of in a halo effect.

Chuckling, Bob says, "Pictures of the birds around Tiger. How cute."

Cute? Arghhh.

"And video," he adds.

Video? She's got video? Of the cackle? Oh I hope not. That's not fair. That's plumb un-American. Shouldn't be legal.

FINE. Just FINE.

No one is paying any attention to me. They are all looking at the stupid video, so I turn my back on everyone.

"Wait. Stop," Bob says to Boston, "Go back to that picture you just skipped over. Is that Ludwig's trailer?"

"Yes. Why?"

"On my way home tonight, Ludwig stopped me

out in front of his trailer. Said people were peeking in his window."

"What?"

"Yeah. Started this morning. Nate parked his car by the side of the road and get out and looked in Lud's window. Then Mary did the same thing. A bunch of people stopped and stared. One of them even used binoculars."

Oh, this should be interesting.

Boston is kind of biting her lower lip.

Maybe her turn to be humiliated?

"What did Lud do? He punch any of them out?" Jackson asks.

"After three people gawked in his window, he pulled the drapes. People kept stopping all day. I told him to give me a call if it happened again and I'd come over."

Boston covers her eyes and forehead with her palms and forefingers.

Her version of disappearing?

Bob finally notices. "Boston?" he says and waits.

"They aren't looking in his window," she sort of whispers.

"They're not?"

Boston moves her hand over her mouth now and her eyes are big. "I never thought. Oh my goodness, I never thought." She shakes her head. "I never noticed. I was so focused on the hummingbirds."

She told me all about her hummingbird stop this morning. She was excited.

"What do hummingbirds have to do with peeping

toms? They're little birds, right? Never mind, we'll come back to hummingbirds. Tell me why people are looking in Lud's window."

"I saw hummingbirds working that hibiscus bush in front of his trailer this morning. Two of them. We don't see them here, and I was excited." She stops. Puts her head down on the table.

Definitely disappearing.

"My fault. His front window is right behind that bush. I never even noticed." She picks her head up and puts her hands in front of her eyes again.

"I might have told a few people about the humming-birds." She puts her forehead down on the table again.

Disappeared.

"And they told people who told other people. And everyone stopped to look for the hummingbirds, you think?" Bob asks.

She nods her head. Her face still on the table. "I never thought. When I told people about the hummingbirds. I never thought. Oh, I have video of the birds. I took a video of them."

"Play it for us," Bob says.

"I'm kind of afraid to. I might have Lud naked in his window. Oh, Bob, tell me he was dressed. Please."

Bob laughs. "Yes, he was. At least when he talked to me. Let's see the video."

They all watch another one of her videos.

"No naked man," she breathes with a sigh of relief when it's over.

"No hummingbirds either," Bob says.

"What do you mean, no hummingbirds? Of course, there are hummingbirds. I forgot to look for birds. I was concentrating on the window hoping not to see a naked Lugwig." She fiddles with her cell. "Here look, I'll show you."

She plays it again. "Out of focus bush. No birds. Not even a bird shape," she says dejectedly.

Guess she can't catch a bird either.

"On the bright side," she finishes with a smile, "no naked man either."

Why couldn't the video of me be out of focus with no birds. Stupid birds.

"Now, tell me about hummingbirds. I'm not sure what they look like," Bob says.

"They're tiny, about four inches long and an inch around. They have very long, skinny beaks to poke into a flower's center to get the nectar. And they come in very bright colors. We have three types in Florida. I couldn't see the colors of these well enough to identify them. Probably ruby throated, it's the most common."

"And they hum?"

No they don't hum. Well, their wings make the humming noise, they beat so fast. So fast you can't see them, Boston told me. I'm not sure I believe that. And they can fly backwards. Big deal. I can walk backwards.

Boston goes into more detail about the birds. She told me all about them when she came home.

I'm leaving.

Where to? I look around. Opt for the seagrape. Climb three feet up the trunk and crawl into the cradle formed by three limbs, curl up in my tree bed, and close my eyes. Not hiding. Just seeking some solitude and quiet to finish my nap.

I've barely shut my eyes when. "Chitter. Chitter. Chitter."

Oh for goodness sake. Now what?

Not chak, chac, chac. Chit chit chit. Conk-la-reeeee. Conk-la-reee. But a skittering. And I can feel someone looking at me.

I repeat the 'open one eye, a sliver width, both inner and outer lid'.

Yoda. Staring at me with his white ears and nose. He chitters.

Is that like a cackle? And what does he want?

He looks up at one of the branches, then at me, and again at the branch. Squeezes past me and climbs further up the tree.

Figures that I'd decide to nap on his route to his nest. Figures.

I'm awake now. Look around. The people are still at the table, talking quietly.

Hmm. Something is moving about halfway to the shore in a clump of tall grass. Huh? I study the spot.

Stopped now.

Shakes again.

No one is paying any attention to me. They are now talking about the BBQ tonight. Kevlar and Bob are cooking burgers and chicken. My favorites. Hot dogs too, but I don't really like those. Jackson says he'll bring Polish sausage. Those are good. They start arguing about sauces. At least they aren't laughing at the red-winged video.

Grass is rustling still. I climb down and mosey over toward the spot. Nothing moving now. But I smell something. Not quite bird? It's kind of strange. I tilt my head to get a better sniff.

I wander closer. Can smell bird now. Yes. Predator.

Can't see what kind of bird. Just a dark shape leaning over, sort of poking at something. It's so focused it doesn't even notice me. Stupid bird.

I reach out a tentative paw and touch a feather.

Realize it is a large feather.

The bird jumps up, turns.

A monster bird. Huge. Towers over me. Lots bigger than a hawk. Stands two feet high with a white head, a wicked yellow beak. Bigger than I am.

Not my day. I pounce on a little bird; it disappears. I gently tap another bird and it becomes a giant.

I lift my paw off his feather. Never take my eyes off his beady yellow eyes.

He stares at me. He flaps a wing. A huge wing.

Oops. I might be in a little trouble here.

He is studying me. Like maybe I'm his next snack?

I fumble back a few steps. Off balance.

Coming over here was a big mistake; I should have stayed safely surrounded by the red-wingeds.

Whatever he was pawing at races off. Lucky him.

The bird towers over me. Threatening. He doesn't blink. I'm sort of frozen.

Twice as tall as me, and as thick around. Brown with that white head and wicked looking beak. Beady yellow eyes stare. Angry.

I show him my eyeteeth.

He shows me a taloned claw.

Gulp.

They look like bear claws. Giant claws.

Pretty sure I'm in a little trouble here.

Boston is yelling. I tilt an ear back toward her but keep looking straight into the monster's eyes. If I look away, I know he will be on me. Not sure I could look away.

"No Tiger," she shouts. "No. Stop. Don't. Come back."

Don't come back? What does she mean?

"No. Don't. Don't hurt him, Tiger."

Me hurt him? How about telling him not to hurt me? Could use a little help here.

The beast turns to glance at Boston.

I can move. I look too. She is running toward us. With Sluggo right behind. She stops about ten feet away. He stops behind her. Howls.

Boston claps her hands and yells, "Scat. Bird. Scat."

The fiend scowls at me. He is not impressed.

I'm on my own.

My mouth is dry. I open it wide. All teeth showing. Roll my tongue and howl my very best angry panther imitation.

"RRRROARRRR."

He jerks his head back.

I snap my tongue against the roof of my mouth, while

growling. Spittle flies off my teeth. I can't seem to stop the noise.

"GRRROWLLLLLRRR"

He blinks.

Spittle lands on his front. He raises his wings. They stretch out forever blocking the sun.

"GRRRRR. YOOWWLL"

He flaps, nearly knocking me over. Lifts into the sky and flies away.

I sink down on my belly and breathe.

Boston runs to me and picks me up and pulls me tight to her chest. Walks slowly back to the others. "What am I going to do?" she asks. "Tiger attacked an endangered bald eagle."

"You saw him do that?" Bob questions her.

"Well, I, um, saw him standing on the eagle's wing. You were right there. You saw it too."

"That's sort of what I saw. You remember the two ways you watched the hummingbird video? First looking at the window? Then studying the bush? What I saw was the eagle threatening him. Getting ready to pick him up and take him to his nest."

Boston splutters at him. "Right. Eagles don't eat cats. They eat squirrels, rabbits, and fish. Not cats. No eagle is going to carry an eighteen-pound cat to its nest."

"Who says?" he asks. "The bald eagle is a big predator. Has a six-to-eight-foot wingspan, stands two to three feet tall. And this one was certainly on the larger side of those estimates."

Kind of funny, Bob telling Boston facts about the bald eagle.

"Who can say he wouldn't try for a cat? He doesn't know how much the cat weighs. The eagle sees that rabbit wandering around in the grass and swoops down on him. Cat comes over and steps on his wing. Rabbit runs off. Bird gets angry. Picks up the cat."

Jackson injects, "If Tiger weighs eighteen pounds, I'll eat my hat. He's twenty if he's an ounce. Besides. I saw a third version. I saw your cat rescue a rabbit from the eagle and then the eagle tried to eat the cat. If anything, Tiger might be guilty of almost feeding the wildlife."

Bob and Jackson bump fists.

No way. That bird couldn't eat me. Besides, I had that guy frozen in fear.

Boston studies both of them. Hugs me again.

"Oh my poor baby," she whispers, her face in my fur. "You almost became an eagle dinner."

Poor baby?

I want to be offended because Maine Coon cats are not 'poor babies' but I still am a little shaky and her touch and words are comforting.

"Let's go inside and get some tuna," she suggests. "Tuna with bacon on top."

Alright! It has been a long, long day, but I am the victor. I whomped that stupid bird without even touching him. Scared him silly.

I hope the turkey is juicy, my mouth is dry.

FORT JEFF

We are going to Fort Jefferson National Park, a group of islands in the Dry Tortugas off the Florida Keys. We're going for a month-long tour of duty. Kevlar is. We're going with him.

Boston says *you* can only get to Fort Jeff by boat or plane because Fort Jeff is an island and an island is land completely surrounded by water.

I know what an island is. Like Cumberland Island. Like the little eagle key we can see from our house.

We are flying. I've flown before. I hate flying. I got lucky on my first trip. We got cancelled. We were going to fly home to Boston, but then we got married and we stayed in Flamingo. The second time we flew out west to Reno. Yuk. Now another island. I don't like water much. Unless it's in my water dish, then it's okay. But to be surrounded by water? I don't think I like that. I don't want to go. Not that I have much choice. Boston grabbed me and shoved me into my traveling case.

Yeah, right, traveling case. Think cage. It's a cage. A rose by any other name is still a cage. At least she put a couple of my toys and my pillow inside. My favorite pillow, purple on one side, tan on the other. She bought it for Kevlar, but I slept on it first, and then he wouldn't touch it. Ha. Ha.

She packed my litter pan too, along with their luggage.

This time we drive to an airfield. Not the airport like when we went out west. And this plane is smaller. This plane is the size of our car but with long wings out the side. A seaplane, she explains, "Sometimes called a float plane. It has wheels and pontoons and can land and take off from land or water. Planes and boats both use nautical terms."

I'm not sure how these terms will affect me, but I'm practicing my relevant listening. Nothing else to do.

"Boating people have their own language," she says. "There are small boats which are called boats; large boats are called ships. The front pointy part is the bow. Spelt b o w, sort of like the bow in bow wow, or the bow in kneel down, not like the bough in a tree."

Are you serious? Guess so, because she continues. "The back squarish part is the stern. The right side, when you're facing the bow, is the star board side."

Star Board? A board with stars? Stupid words.

"The left side is the port side."

And I need to know all these terms because?

Kevlar adds, sort of snorting. "You need to know those terms, Tiger, so if a cat falls over the side of a boat into the water at the fort, you can yell cat overboard, port side."

That is not funny. I don't need to be reminded of the time I fell off the side of the boat and would have drowned if Kevlar had not rescued me.

I glare at him.

"The kitchen is the galley; the bathroom is the head."

He's making it up now.

Boston continues, "All the words are old, from Latin and Greek. Like nautical, which means sea or water." She spells it.

What does all this have to do with the plane? Do they have star boards?

Boston leans over me. "You will have your own seat, Tiger. Kev will put the cooler under your cat cage, um cat grotto, so you can see out the window. You can't sit in my lap. You have to stay in the cage, a, um, grotto. Miles is afraid you might explore and get mixed up with the plane pedals."

Humph. I turn my back on her and clean my tail.

Miles is the pie-let. Whatever that is. Not a small pie. A person. Don't know how any kind of pie guy can decide where I sit. And what does she mean by pedals? Like a bicycle?

Miles points at me. "How much does that animal weigh? Must run thirty pounds," he asks. "He's huge. Tough looking."

Always did like Miles. I am tough. And strong. And smart. But thirty pounds? I close my eyes and snort. Any respectable Maine Coon cat weighs at least fifteen pounds.

Even a disrespectable Coon cat. I think I'm between fifteen and twenty. I smile at him.

Kevlar puts our luggage, two duffels, and my litter pan, in the storage compartment. They sent the big suitcases, groceries, and coolers ahead by the boat. At least we don't have to go on the boat, though Boston says, it's pretty big. Not big enough to be called a ship. We may have to come home on it when our tour of duty is over.

Is that a threat?

Miles is busy checking all his little round things in the front. Revs the engine. I lay my ears back at the sound. We start down the street and soon my stomach goes, urp, and I'm pressed down and to the back of the cage as the engine revs even louder and the trees whip by. And it's very noisy.

After a few moments, all my inner parts settle back where they belong, and the noise level lowers. Some.

I don't like the way my stomach fell. And then raised to my backbone. And it keeps repeating as the plane goes up, down. Boston says the plane is hitting rough patches, falling in the downdrafts, rising on the updrafts. Sigh.

Kevlar is riding up front with Miles because he is working during the flight, counting the boats in the backcountry for Resource Management. Kevlar marks the locations of the boats on a map, chart, Boston calls it. A map of the ocean is a chart, she says. Always teaching. Boston and I have the back two seats.

Miles hands Boston some black things and motions for her to put them on her head and yells, "You need these on if you want to talk with us over the engine noise; you need the headphones to block out the sound."

Oh, I could use those.

She puts the round things over her ears and adjusts a little black thing by her mouth. Kevlar and Miles do the same.

I can see out my window, but there's nothing out there and the window is foggy. I peek out the window on the other side of Boston. Same scene as out mine. Nothing. White. Boring.

"Clouds," she says.

She expects me to believe I'm high up in the sky in the clouds like a bird. Not that she has ever lied to me, but really. Nothing out the window but clouds. Right outside the window. All over. Nothing else, just clouds as far as I can see. Even when I look down under us. The trees disappear and there are only white clouds!

Kevlar has his tablet out and starts talking into his microphone and tapping his screen. I can't hear the words over the engine noise.

Wish I could block out the sound too.

Now I can see out and I don't like it. Water. Under us. But far far away. Makes me nervous so I don't look down. Told you I was smart. I'm bored, so I catnap. Until the plane makes a turn and we sort of tilt sideways.

"There's the fort, Tiger," Boston says pointing out the window

Directly down out the window.

I don't see a fort. Only the outside walls of a building.

Six outside walls with an open area in the center. The walls circle the whole island except for a small beach. Was it destroyed? Boston didn't say it was destroyed.

Suddenly, I slide to the front of the cage and my insides jump up in my throat. I scrabble for a hold. The plane is heading down, nose first. It hits the ground. With a splash.

"We've landed," she says.

Safely? I guess so, no one is panicking. Except me. We landed on the WATER. And now I'm on a boat.

We float and motor to the beach where Miles opens a door, steps out.

The air is full of fresh smells. Sea. And sand too.

"Fort Jefferson National Monument," Boston says as she steps out and reaches back in for me. She carries me out the door and over water. I press myself into the back of the cage until she sets me down on the beach.

Whew. I hate water and am still too close. The waves are only a few short feet in front of me. I watch them carefully.

They're not getting closer. So, okay. Maybe.

A crab runs across the sand, and I turn to watch it. There are two, no three of them. Skittering, with their claws waving. Might be fun here.

Where are you Boston? Are you going to open my door?

A short hunched over man strides down the beach. "Hey, now, folks," he says. "Welcome to Ft. Jeff," and he holds out his hand. "Kev. Glad to have you back on board. Really need you to get the refurbishment project moving." He turns to Boston and adds, "Dr. Teddy Roose. Call me

Teddy. It's a pleasure to have you ma'am, heard some tall stories. Hehehe."

He starts to turn away.

"Merow?"

"Oh. That's right. There is a cat." He bends over to look at me. "Um. It will have to stay indoors during the day when visitors are here."

It? He's calling me an it?

"Guess it will be okay for it to be out after hours. It can't get lost because we close the gates at dusk so it can't leave the compound. No place for it to go anyhow, unless it swims. Hehehe. That's what made FOJO, Fort Jeff, such a good prison. Surrounded by water."

"He," Boston tells him.

"Oh, sorry."

You should be sorry.

"Is it, he, a mouser? We could use one. The black rat population has exploded, we're always trying to keep them in check. He could catch rats."

Rats? I can chase rats? Is that what he's saying? I might like it here. Crabs and rats. That daytime lockup thing isn't going to last long.

"No, Tiger is not a hunter. Likes his food taken out of a can and placed in his dish."

I can hunt.

Roose dips his head. "Oh, well. Too bad. The rats, Rattus rattus, are creating havoc with the campers. Tearing up camping gear to get to the food. Doesn't matter how many signs we put up, how many times we warn people.

They still seem to have to have that box of cookies by their pillow. Hehehe."

Boston shakes her head and picks up my cage. "We have a similar problem at Flamingo, but with raccoons. We post suggestions, on how to pack your food away, but there are always those who don't pay attention and, if a rule can be misinterpreted, it is."

"Right," Roose agrees. He reaches to grab the saddle-bags Miles hands him. "Special delivery from Headquarters and Key West. Get your gear and I'll show you to your quarters. Follow along."

Where? The walls are full of holes.

We head toward a flat wooden bridge which crosses over some more water. Moat, Boston called the water. Three men walk toward us, each carrying a small duffle.

Roose says, "Some seasonals are going back with Miles on leave. Vacation. He's dropping them at Key West."

One stops to talk with Kevlar. "Should be a shrimper come in tomorrow. Good guy. Will trade heads-on shrimp for beer. Got some?"

Shrimp?

"You bet. Brought it special for trading. Keep a few for myself. You staying in Key West?"

"Four days. Got a buddy puts us up."

The men head for the plane.

Dr. Teddy says, "We're having a BBQ on the beach later tonight. Fish and shrimp. Hotdogs and hamburgers."

Ohh, yeah, my favorites. Fish and shrimp. Hamburgers. Hot dogs are okay too. This is a great place.

We walk through the giant gate. There is a large house across the way in an open grassy yard.

I guess we are staying there.

"That's my residence on the parade ground. I have it all to myself right now. The wife is vacationing up north," he tells Boston.

Parade ground? Parades are noisy? Back home parades are in the street. I don't see any floats. Where are the rats. Hmm.

"You two will be inside the fort, in one of the casements," he says leading us across the courtyard and into the brick building. The one with all the holes in the walls.

Casement? What is a casement?

"I've put you in dormitory one; it has three bedrooms, two bathrooms and a common area. The main bedroom has a private bath. You don't have to share the bunkhouse though, the area is all yours. Hehehe."

We walk through a large arched brick entranceway into a dark corridor. It's chilly and damp and smells old and musty. Small bulbs in the ceiling give off meager light. Not that I need light, but humans do. We walk through a normal door and into our temporary home.

The place is clean, but the floor has sand over it. But there are holes in the walls here too.

Kevlar puts the laptops on the desk in the square common room. Boston sets my case down, unzipping the flap. I step out slowly and stretch.

She pulls out my dishes, puts water in one and a snack in the other. And I'm torn between eating and exploring and catching rats. Black rats or kibble. Not shrimp. Oh well. I eat a few nuggets and cover the rest, so they won't go bad. Time to check the place out.

I search the dormitory and check all the corners. Two rooms have bunkbeds, those top ones might be fun. The third room, ours, is larger and has only one bed.

"That's pretty cool," Boston says going to one of the wall holes. "Our very own cannon gun-port windows."

Is that a nautical term? Left. Port? I can see the ocean through the gun ports.

I don't smell rats. I jump on top of the dresser to watch Boston empty the duffle and put clothes in drawers. Then I follow Kevlar to the bathroom where he sets out my litter box and fills it.

Good.

"Let's go explore," he says. "I want to show you Mudd's cell and some cannon, then we can wander down to the dock and beach." Kevlar worked at the fort before and knows his way around.

I'm not sure why we want to go look at someone's muddy cellphone, but I'm game. I hope the BBQ has started.

Boston pulls out my harness and has it on before I realize what she's doing.

What? I don't need that.

Kevlar smirks. "It's just until you learn your way around, Tiger. We don't want you wandering off and falling into a cistern."

Hump. Like I would do that. I flatten my eyes at him. *What's a cistern? Maybe I want to fall in one.*

"Don't tease him, Kev," Boston says, and explains, "The cisterns are large holes where water is collected and stored and they're all covered. You don't have to worry about falling into one." She attaches the leash to my harness, and we head out into the corridor.

Well, they do. I sit. *Not going anywhere with a harness on.*

She picks me up and carries me down the hall.

Huh. That didn't work quite the way I planned.

We walk down the damp corridor to an open small square empty room with three very tall skinny windows.

"Dr. Mudd's cell," Boston says.

It's a cell. Not a muddy cellphone. A cage. A human cage. Like a cat carrying case, but lots larger. Wait. It doesn't have a door. How can it be a cage without a door?

"A casement, or casemate, actually, for a cannon," Kevlar explains. "This was a fortified gunroom when the fort was first built so it didn't have a door. Until it became a prison."

Casement. Casemate. Tomato. Tomahto. Not sure I care. And it's not muddy. It is a small, chilly, brick room. Not just chilly, but cold and damp. Brick and cement. The ceiling has little white icicles hanging from it. Kevlar calls them stalactites and says they are made from the moisture dissolving the cement and mortar. The walls have cone shaped drips of the same mortar. "And it has trenches and pits dug in the floor to drain rainwater," he tells us.

I know cement, but what is mort r?

I walk around but don't find any sign of rats. No smell or droppings either. There's nothing to play with or eat. Not even the smell of food. It's a big empty damp room.

I tap a smudge on the wall with my paw and the mort r crumbles. Some white bits get stuck between my pads. Icky.

Boston paraphrases the plaque she's reading. "Dr. Mudd. With two ds. Mudd was a doctor who was locked up here for three years because he treated John Wilkes Booth after Wilkes shot President Lincoln. After the civil war."

Civil war? I must have misunderstood that. A civil – friendly – war?

Boston's still reading. "Because he helped people here at the fort, and saved prisoners and staff from yellow fever, he was pardoned and allowed to go home."

About the only part I understand is the prisoner part because that's what I am when they lock me up in the carrying case. And this harness I have on makes me a prisoner. I know about the pardoned part too, because Boston pardons me all the time.

"I always think of him as innocent," she says, pacing around the cell following me. "No one proved he knew Booth had shot the president. Mudd treated John Wilkes Booth because Mudd was a doctor. There was not much evidence verifying that he was involved in the assassination, and Mudd showed he was a dedicated doctor when he saved all those soldiers from yellow fever. Saved the very same men who kept him locked in this cell."

Kevlar nods. "There are groups of people out there who agree with you. Unfortunately, we'll never know."

I'm bored. I could nap but I don't dare lay myself

down. That mortar stuff will stick to me like beggar lice. I hate beggar lice. Now I'm a prisoner in this mud cell.

Finally, they are through looking at this room.

Really, really interesting. Not.

We head for the ram parts or ramp arts. I'm not sure which. Boston hasn't explained. I forget that I'm sulking, and I lead the way with my tail up, pulling them back up the corridor with my leash.

"I keep forgetting. Is ramparts the flat top of the fort wall? With the walkway?" Boston asks Kevlar.

"Yeah. The canons sit on the broad embankment at the top and are also set within the walls. They're spaced so that many of them can be aimed at the same target. The soldiers heated the cannon balls in the furnace, loaded them into the canon, and fired them. The hot balls hit the ships and set the wood on fire. Kind of cool," he said with a smile. "They didn't need to hole the ships to sink them."

This was the civil war?

We head up a small hill to the top of the fort wall, rampart, and Boston sits on a cannon. It smells of old black iron. I sniff around in the grass, but don't find anything and jump up with Boston on top of the cannon. Walk along the top, crouch down and look through the front mouth. Hmm. Old rat nest. Wonder if I need to scramble in and sniff closer.

Before I can decide, Teddy finds us.

"Amazing spot, isn't it? Nature on the big screen." He faces out looking over the ocean. A small island in the distance. Birds are soaring far out there. Black ones with very long thin wings.

"I try to come up once a day to take in the ocean and clouds and the fort. Nothing for miles and miles except a few small islands. And the magnificent frigate birds soaring. The quiet. Makes me feel small and unimportant. Hehehe." He turns in a full circle.

"It makes me marvel at the ability of man. How did they know in eighteen hundred and forty-six, that this channel was the perfect spot to build a fort to control shipping or block warships? They didn't have airplanes or satellites to map the area. And they built the fort, one brick at a time. All by hand, no heavy equipment. Only slaves and soldiers."

They stand quietly for a few moments and watch a boat, or is it a ship, make its way into the harbor.

The boat comes near the finger pier and misses it, ricocheting off. Tries again and bumps it hard and bounces off. Tries again and doesn't make any contact and goes around for another attempt.

"Novice boater," Roose says. "I sometimes wonder how they ever make it out here. Especially a yacht that size." He shakes his head. Then points to a second vessel with nets hanging from tall poles. "Shrimper."

Ohh. Shrimp. My favorite. I'm ready.

"Not an active shrimper. The tangled nets with the holes are a dead giveaway," he adds as the shrimper comes alongside the dock and three men hop off with lines. Not ropes. Only ropes for landlubbers. Lines for seamen. That's what Kevlar told me and Boston.

Not active? No shrimp?

Roose says, "Neither of those boats is scheduled to be here."

We watch the yacht make two more tries and then the three men from the shrimper motion for the yacht to toss lines. They grab them and drag the boat to the pier.

Roose points to two small dots, farther out to sea. "Coast Guard cutters, heading this way. Probably not a coincidence, them here at the same time as an out of service shrimper. I better go down and take a closer look. Hehehe. Think I'll give my men a heads-up." He pulls out his park short-wave radio and calls for backup.

We walk down the hill together to the parade ground and I follow them across the wooden bridge to the finger pier.

Men lift three giant coolers off the shrimper to the dock and open one. Two men from the other boat are looking inside the cooler and arguing with the shrimpers. Boston wanders over and peeks in over their shoulders. I have to go with her, because she still has my leash.

"Oh, wow. Shrimp."

Really? Shrimp? They have shrimp? I take three steps around the men. It's a tall cooler and I have to stand on my hind legs and rest my paws on the top edge of the cooler to peek over.

Wow. Yes. Shrimp. It's filled with shrimp. The cooler is huge. They'll never miss a few. No one is watching me.

I reach a few and scratch them out over the side. Almost picture myself rolling in them.

Boston asks one of the shrimpers, "Are you selling these to the folks on the motorboat? Can we buy some, too? Or maybe buy them from the motorboat?"

Her eyes are really wide and innocent. Didn't know she could do that. Don't know what she's up to, but that look means she is up to something. The look is like the one I do when she catches me doing something bad. All wide eyed, who me? innocent.

The man blocks her view of the cooler. "Not for sale, lady."

Bummer. But while everyone is gathered around her and

not paying attention to me, I reach in with my paw and scrape more shrimp to the side of the cooler. Give a quick look around. Scoop them out, onto the dock down in front of me. Head on and all skinny legs like Kevlar's bait shrimp.

"Just a small bag, maybe?" Boston pleads, "Please?"

I snag more.

I have myself a nice little pile. Crouch down, bite one. Crunch.

Crunch? It still has its shell and its cold. Frozen. Huh? I sniff it. Old. Really old. Do I really care if they are old? No. They don't smell bad.

One of the men, wearing a business suit which you don't see too often near water, screams at me. "Hey. Get away from there. Stupid cat."

I try my innocent who me? look. But it's hard to pull off with a shrimp in my mouth.

He lashes out with a shiny black pointy shoe.

I'm too quick and jump back out of his reach. He misses.

He raises his leg to kick me again and Kevlar puts a restraining hand on the guy's shoulder twisting him away from me. "Don't kick the cat," Kevlar tells him in a dangerous tone which I have never heard.

Wow. I back up out of the way.

They stare at each other. The other guys stop their conversation and crowd around. The air is full of tension and threat.

"Who do you think you are, Buddy," the kicker shouts at Kevlar.

Roose stomps to us followed by one of his men. "He's a Park Ranger, mister. Back off." Roose has his hand on the weapon in his holster and pushes between them, facing the kicker.

While everyone is distracted, I reach in for more shrimp, but can't feel any and when I peek over the edge, I see white square-shaped bags.

Bummer. A thin layer of old frozen shrimp covered the bags. Yukky.

I consider my pile. Shrimp in shells. At home Boston takes the shell off for me. I look up toward her. The second ranger is staring into my cooler. He reaches in and shoves the remaining shrimp aside, the ones I couldn't reach. Brushes them over the edge to land in front of me.

Ohh, yes. More for me.

"What do we have here," he says pulling out a white bag. He holds it up. "Roose?"

Roose glances over and into the cooler. "Well, well, well. Hehehe. That looks mighty like contraband."

The man wearing the suit says "Just walk away, mister, and no one gets hurt. We're just making a little transfer here."

We all look at him.

"We're making a private transaction here. None of your business. So walk away. We don't want any trouble." He nods toward the shrimper where men are holding rifles and looking our way.

"Not happening, buddy. Hehehe," Roose says. Gives Kevlar a microscopic nod and Kevlar pulls the man in front of himself, twisting his arm behind his back.

Roose pulls his own weapon.

"Just relax everyone," Roose suggests.

But I am ready to run. Not away. I'm a brave Maine

Coon cat, we don't run away. But we're smart enough to know when to leave. I don't like the noise guns can make. It hurt my ears.

Roose waves one arm into the air. Two Coast Guard cutters approach with loud sirens. **Whoop. Whoop. Whoop.** Overhead is a deafening chopper.

My ears hurt and I lay them down flat.

Roose is yelling at the men on the dock to get down and the two Coast Guard cutters, sirens wailing, pull alongside. Sailors jump aboard the two docked boats and cuff the men.

Before I can run, Boston snatches me up and takes me off the dock, out of the way. I don't have time to grab my shrimp, but I keep an eye on my pile. She cuddles me close to her shoulder and we watch the activity.

The Coasties and Rangers are arresting all the men. And the Coasties lead the prisoners onboard the cutters, then Boston carries me over to Kevlar, Roose, and the Coast Guard Captain.

Roose says, "They're drug smugglers. The shrimper had the drugs hidden in the coolers under the shrimp. They were offloading the drugs to the yacht which was going to take them to Key West."

The Coast Guard captain says, "We've been tagging that shrimper for two days. This morning that yacht tried to tie up alongside it on the water." He laughs. "Nearly sank both boats. Guess they decided to try your docks. We're confiscating everything, boats, coolers, even the kitty's pile of shrimp, Sorry, Kitty," he says to me.

Kitty? He called me Kitty? And is taking my shrimp? I narrow my eyes at him. Lay my ears back this time in a threat.

"Don't like that, hunh?" he says. "Well, maybe we can find you some fresh shrimp in our cooler, because you made our job a bit easier today."

Okay.

"Maybe, a nice piece of fish too."

Oh. Fish and shrimp. My favorite.

Wait. What about BBQ on the beach?

PRINCESS

Boston asks Kevlar, "Remember what happened that day I took Tiger to work?"

I do. It was great. I got lots of attention and snacks from campers and staff. I harassed a lizard. Helped with a drug bust and got a fish dinner.

She stands waiting for him to answer.

I stretch from my nap, walk toward her to remind her. *You're supposed to get me supper, not stand and question Kevlar.*

"You mean your infamous Take Your Cat to Work Day?" he responds. "When you and Tiger helped the Rangers catch those dope smugglers and make the biggest drug bust ever?"

Yeah. Told ya. I did it. I helped. Me. It was cool. The humans hunted in a pack.

"Remember how it started?" Boston asks.

"You had a feeling, a sixth sense, a clairvoyant moment," he replies and stops. "Don't tell me you have another feeling. And if so, why wait until you come home from work? Why didn't you call your buddy Ranger Bob? Claire?"

Claire is a nickname they use for her now, because she senses things. Like she spotted the dope smugglers. I'm pretty sure Claire is kind of a compliment. They still call her Boston, because that's where we are from. Her and me. We met Kevlar here. Kevlar is the name I call him. Everyone else calls him Kev.

Boston answers as she heads into the kitchen. Oh, good she's getting my supper. I wander after her. "Bob went to town. He'll be back soon," she says. "But I saw something weird. Gave me a feeling."

"Tell me about this feeling. Another wrong guy like the last time?"

Yay, she has my food dish and a can of cat food.

"Not wrong. More weird. Off. Acting. That's what it felt like. He was playing a part. Why would he do that? Why would anyone play a part to impress a campground teller? Why would I care? All I'm interested in is the camper comes in, pays for a space, and parks."

Kevlar nods slowly, looking puzzled. "So he's acting. That worries you?"

She's worried? I'm the one who's worried. Who cares about weird campers? They're all weird. I'm worried because she stopped filling my dish.

The real problem here is my supper, people.

She turns around and faces him, leaving the can and my dish on the counter. Waving a spoon with my turkey bacon on it.

Supper, Boston. My supper.

She points the spoon at Kevlar. "Here's the way it went. This couple came in with this brand new sixty-foot camper. Fifth wheel. Fancy rig. Top of the line. Towed by an old pickup truck. A couple. Older guy, younger woman. Both slightly off."

She shakes the spoon to emphasize the point and a dollop of food flies off and sticks on Kevlar's shirt. Too far up for me to get. She puts the spoon down, gets a paper towel and picks it off and throws it in the sink.

What? That's mine. I could eat that. That was part of my supper.

I send outraged thoughts to her.

Supper Boston. My supper.

"MEROW?"

"Oh, Tiger. I'm sorry. I forgot you," she says, looking down at me.

Forgot me? Me?

She turns back and spoons food into my bowl. Kevlar rubs the wet spot on his shirt and Boston continues with her story. "Cute couple. And they are a couple. No doubt in my mind. They're not playacting the couple part. But…"

She closes the can and puts it in the refrigerator. Rinses off the spoon. Turns back to Kevlar.

"GRRR."

This is getting to be too much.

Supper Boston. You'd think if she were clairvoyant, she'd be getting the message.

"Oh, okay Tiger." She puts my dish down.

Finally. I better eat it before she forgets and takes it away. And it's my favorite. Bacon with turkey.

"So, a couple. May/December. But campers? No way. Had trouble unhitching the truck. And then couldn't level the camper. Had to get out instructions." She snorts.

"You said it was a new rig. New enough they don't know all the workings yet," Kevlar suggests reasonably.

"Yes, yes, yes. But then they came over and asked weird questions."

"Like?"

"A lot of people live here? Go back and forth to town often?"

"They might just be curious. What else?"

"When does the marina open? We need milk for our coffee. When's sunrise."

"Why's that weird?"

"Well, you'd think they would just go to the marina today if they want milk for their coffee in the morning. And get this, they are carrying fly-fishing poles." She har-rumphs. "Fly fishing? In Flamingo? They didn't even seem to realize no one fly fishes."

"Meoww?" Since we're still in the kitchen, maybe I can get seconds.

Boston looks down at my empty dish. "You just ate. Take your toy." She tosses down a catnip mouse. My turn to snort, but I pick it up and jump on the chair near Kevlar.

"And then they asked for bait. I asked what kind they wanted, and the woman said the live kind." Boston raises her palm and turns it up. "And they looked at each other as if that was an important piece of information. So, okay. I tell them the marina gets regular deliveries. They wanted to know when. And I said, as needed. Then I asked if they had a license and that confused them. I added for fishing."

"So they're learning to camp and fish."

"They don't have a clue about either one."

"What, you think maybe they stole the trailer?"

"Don't get that vibe."

"Want me to drive by, check them out?" he offered. "Though I'm not sure I would spot anything you missed."

"Would you? I can go along."

"No. Better if I go by myself. Won't take long."

We wait. She sits. I play, and I'm still playing with my toy when he comes back. She races to the door to meet him.

"Well? Did you see what I meant?"

He frowns. "I know him," Kevlar says.

"You know him?"

"Met him once even. At my cousin's inn. My cousin's husband's father."

She blinks. "Inn? Cousin who? Husband who? I'm confused. Wait. Inn on Main, on the west coast near Naples. Your cousin, Liz, whose family owns the Inn on Main. Her husband, Calvin, Colin something. His father?"

"Right. Colin. Gibbs. His father. Ryan Gibbs. That's who the man is."

"Then he's okay? My camper is okay? I'm not clairvoyant."

Kevlar doesn't answer right away, and I toss my mouse into the air and catch him.

"Oh, no," she says disappointedly. "You're going to tell me he's not with his wife."

I'm watching them both now, the toy hanging in my paw.

"That could explain my feeling," she groans.

"It's his wife. I've seen their wedding picture."

"Did you stop and talk?"

"No."

"Why? And why are you nervous now?"

"He's a cop. FBI."

"So?"

Kevlar sort of collapses on the couch and she sits beside him. I take my mouse over and drop it on his foot. Pounce on it, accidentally grabbing his foot. He doesn't seem to notice.

"So, I'm wondering what they're doing on the east coast when they have the run of my cousin's inn on the west coast. I'm thinking he might be undercover. It would explain your feeling. I phoned my cousin and asked her to have him call me. Told her to mention who we are and where we live and what we do. That we have a mutual friend, Agent Sanders."

Agent Sanders is my FBI buddy.

"She's some sort of law enforcement too, the wife," he adds.

His cell rings and he checks it. "Undisclosed." He puts it on speaker and answers. "Kev, here."

"Hey Kev. Ryan Gibbs. Liz said I should call you?"

"Right. My wife checked you into the campground.

Thought there was something off. So I swung by your site. Didn't stop because I was concerned you might be working." He pauses a moment. "If you're not working, we'd like to invite you to dinner." Boston nods at him. "Fish fry."

"Sound good. But we are working. Can we meet someplace public? Casually bump into each other? Say in fifteen minutes?" Ryan asks.

"Campground, walk-in tent camping. We can be at a picnic table. My wife sketches."

"Sounds good. I hear there is a cat too. Maybe bring him."

Cat? Me? I get to go? Will there be shrimp?

"We can do that."

"In a bit then."

Kevlar disconnects and looks at Boston. "Bring the wife, the sketching, the cat. Gives him an excuse to stop and talk."

"He can't be working in the park; we'd know. Well, the rangers would know. If they know, one of them would have told us. I'm confused," Boston says.

"One way to get unconfused. Gather your stuff."

She packs up her sketch pad and pencils. Gets my carrier. Throws some snacks in and motions me inside.

I look over at her and blink. *I don't need a carrier. I sit in the middle of the front seat of the truck.*

"Okay. But we bring the carrier because we'll be in a public place. If you are good, maybe you get some shrimp." She picks me up and I let her because she said the magic word. Shrimp. Kevlar picks up the carrier and her sketch stuff and we're out the door.

And I ride in the middle of the front seat between the two of them.

At the campground, Boston groans and motions out the window at a van parked on the grass under a tree. "That guy. I've had nothing but trouble from him for a week. Always just barely over the illegal line. Always has to park his van in the shade. And the shade he wants is always on the grass. And now he has his tent over near there too, instead of at his assigned site. Got a good mind to go give him a ticket."

Kevlar parks by a table. "Maybe after we meet with Ryan and his wife. And you go home and change back into your uniform," he suggests.

She grimaces. "You're right. I'm just grumbling. But my ticket finger is itchy."

Boston puts on my harness with the pink leash and carries me to a picnic table in the shade of a palm tree. "Stay on the table," she says setting me down.

Maybe. I check out the area. Some people are launching a kayak down by the shoreline. Seagulls flap around them looking hopeful. Kevlar strolls over to watch.

A man walks by us and frowns when he sees me. I frown back and he moves on. Two people on bicycles slow down. The woman points at me and stops and dismounts and comes to our table. The man wanders over to talk to Kevlar.

"A Maine Coon cat," she says in an awed tone.

This is one smart lady. I sit taller.

"What a beautiful handsome cat. I'll bet you are brave and bold and a great hunter," she says to me.

I smile. *That's right. A brave hunter.* Just being honest. Not vain.

She reaches out a hand and I give her a warning glare. *No touching.*

"May I pat, you?" she asks politely keeping her hand where I can see it. It smells faintly of tuna.

Me, she asks. Not Boston.

"Be good," Boston whispers and holds her breath.

She smells good and not just of tuna, but inside. She has a gentle feel and I blink a yes and dip an ear. She extends two fingers of her tuna hand to stroke me.

"What a magnificent cat you are," the smart lady says. She's nice. Her eyes are wide and kind. I shut my own a moment and bask in the warmth.

Open them to give a quick glance at Boston. *This is how you should be looking at me.*

"So soft," the lady whispers watching me closely, same as I'm watching her. "One more time?" she asks, and I stay still so she can stroke me again.

Boston says, "He usually doesn't let anyone touch him."

I don't. But this lady is special.

"His name is Tiger, though mostly I call him Stop or Don't do that. I'm Boston." She holds out her hand in the friendly human gesture, and they grasp and shake.

"Becca. That's my husband Ryan over there." She nods toward Kevlar. "Can I give him a snack? Not Ryan, Tiger."

Oh, I love this lady. *Of course, you can.*

Boston gives her a package of treats, and she pours one out on the table for me. I lean down and pick it up gently, chewing as I watch hoping for more.

I am such a good cat.

She drops three more on the table.

All right. Yes.

Kevlar and Ryan come to sit with us, and Becca introduces her husband.

"What did we do wrong?" Ryan asks Boston.

"It was not so much that you did anything wrong. Just off. You didn't know what you were doing, and it just didn't feel like you were novices. More like you were playing a part. Without a script. You didn't fit. But don't worry. I don't think anyone else would notice."

"Neither of us has ever camped, didn't know there was a special way to do it. How did you find out who we were? Did you run us or something? The tag? That would have come back to the owner of the pickup."

"No. I told Kev I felt uneasy, so he drove to the campground to check you out."

"Because you felt uneasy?" Becca asks surprised.

"A few months ago, I felt uneasy about some campers, and we made a big drug bust."

"Yeah, Agent Sanders told us about that. Called you Claire. Good work. Still doesn't explain how you found out who we are."

"Kev recognized you. He met you at his cousin's inn.

Ryan laughs and shakes his head. "Small world."

I could have another treat.

"You are working then?" Boston says.

"Yeah. Last minute thing. Scuttlebutt saying something going down today. Here in the campground. We were the only ones available. Borrowed the camper, but we didn't have time for a backstory."

"Why come at all? You could have called the rangers. They could do the surveillance."

Boston's a ranger. Sort of.

She continues, "Rangers normally handle any problems in the park, and they work with the FBI frequently because the park is federal property. FBI agents don't generally show up in person. And no one notified the rangers."

They didn't tell the Rangers?

Becca grimaces. "The information mentions a local person doing the deal."

"No way. Not any of us." Boston is quick to defend our Park Service buddies.

Not us. We're the good guys.

Becca shrugs. "Someone working here is selling illegal merchandise. Today. Here. That is all we know."

"Someone who works here is pretty broad. Could include anyone who lives here, commutes, makes deliveries," Boston suggests.

Yeah. And what about my snacks? Anyone? No one is petting me or feeding me. Everyone is ignoring me. Humph.

There is a strange crackling buzzing sound coming from the van Boston was grumbling about. Near it. Sort of a familiar sound. Sort of like large crickets but louder.

Something else too. A chittering. Silly word chittering. Chattering, too. The words don't quite describe the sounds.

Curious. I know that sound but can't place it.

I slip down to the bench seat. No one notices. So I jump to the ground and trot over to the van.

The sound is like a swarm of angry bees. Don't want to mess with bees. I stop and point my ears and listen.

Not bees. Rattles. The sound is rattles. Not in the trees. Must be under the van. Multiple rattles. Rattles is a good word, sounds like a rattle.

There's a smell too. A stink. Rattlesnake stink. So rattlesnake. That's what I hear. Rattlesnakes. More than one.

I edge carefully closer. Not too close, because Boston told me rattlers can strike half their length. Don't want to get within striking distance. One more careful step.

The sounds aren't coming from around the van. I tilt my head. The sounds are coming from inside the van. Rattles and that strange chittering noise.

Another careful step closer and I reach one paw up on the sill. Peek cautiously inside.

Burlap bags. Glass terrariums. Wire cages. They sit on the shelves which line the walls.

A burlap sack moves. Kind of rolls. Lumps inside another sack move.

Wow. I can't decide if I should pounce on the moving sack or one of the lumps. I think a moving lump. I want to grab one of those moving lumps. Yes. Cool. But there are a bunch of those lumps. I have to pick one.

Oops.

The rattle noises are coming from the bags, and the stink is rattlesnake all the way. The moving shapes must be rattlesnakes. Not sure I want to pounce on a rattler, even if it is in a sack. Can they attack through a sack?

I rethink the pounce and instead check out the inside of the van.

The chittering is coming from three glass terrariums. I put both front paws on the sill and lean in. Gators. Baby gators. Crawling over each other and hissing and grunting. Baby gators in terrariums? Baby gators live in pods with a mother gator. Not pods like the hard-shelled Mahogany tree seedpod. More like a pod of whales in the water, except baby gators live in a dry nest near the water. Not that I have ever seen a nest. But I have heard the baby gators.

Other cages hold land crabs, tree snails. Small mice, rats? Things I don't recognize. Everglades wildlife. And two squirrels. One real tiny. The other looks like my buddy Yoda, the mangrove squirrel. He reaches up a paw and presses it against the glass. Chitters at me.

It's not fair. They don't belong in a cage. I don't like them in a cage.

A new sound. An angry hissing. Howling. Growling. Coming from the metal mesh cage on the front seat.

"What's Tiger doing?" Becca asks.

Huh. My left ear twitches back at her as I study the cage. It has a cat smell. And the howling sounds like a cat not a snake. A cat with a sore throat and an accent. I jump up on the door windowsill. Sniff again.

Cat in the cage? Strange cat.

"Grrrrrr." No one should put a cat in a locked cage.

I reach a paw to the seat top.

"Tiger," Boston yells. "Stop. What are you doing?"

No way. I am checking out this cage with the cat.

I put both paws on the seat and peer down. Sniff. Cat. I can see it better now. Not marked like any cat I've ever known. Strange coloring. Kind of a gray or silver. Has striped legs and tail. Dirty. The gray face has a black mask. Green, green eyes. Regal green eyes. Staring at me as if to say, 'what are you waiting for, get me out of here, I can't reach the latch'.

She paws at the lock from the inside. Shows me where it is. Shows me she can't fit her paw through the wiring, only her claws. Has left claw marks on the lock.

I jump on the seat, reach over, and push the latch down. Boston tugs on my pink yarn leash.

Oh oh.

The cat shoves open the cage door, and Boston leans in the window and snatches me out of the van.

"What are you doing? Not yours. Get out of there," she orders and tightens her grip on me and sniffs. "Is that rattlesnake stink. Is there a snake under the van?" She takes a quick step back.

Her face wrinkles up. "That's coming from inside. A rattlesnake inside the van?"

She puts a bracing arm under my back legs, hands me to Becca. "Careful, he's mean," she warns, but I just nuzzle Becca's neck and watch Boston poke her head in the window.

"Burlap bags with something moving inside. Those sacks are good for carrying snakes. Rattlers. You can tell by the stink. Nothing smells like rattler," Boston says and then scans the inside of the van.

"And snake catching sticks. And traps. Terrariums with baby gators. Takes a brave idiot to snatch a baby gator from its mama's nest." She pauses, still looking around the van. "I think that's a flying squirrel. Never seen a live one, but I hear they are being trafficked. And a Mangrove squirrel. Rats, a mole."

She turns. "This is it, Becca. This is the deal you're here for."

Becca and I move up beside her, and Becca points

with her chin. "Rifle barrel sticking out from under the front seat."

"Illegal in the Park. Means we can search."

Do I get one chance at the moving sacks.

I lean down and put my front feet back on the sill.

"Oh, no you don't," Boston says grabbing me back from Becca who pulls out her cell phone and takes pictures.

"Oops," Boston whispers, "Angry man coming." And then in a louder voice she yells, "Don't worry. I got the cat. He didn't get away. I got kitty."

She turns and puts her mouth at my ear. "You're a good cat. Good kitty.

Huh? Where? Me? Well. Okay. I should get a snack then.

Becca says loudly. "Oh, thank goodness. I was afraid he'd get lost and get eaten. Stand there and I'll get some pictures of you and Tiger by the palm trees." Lowers her voice and adds, "And the license plate."

"Good kitty," Boston says louder.

The angry man who was stomping toward us, slows and stops, watches.

Boston whispers, "He's stopped. Just watching now."

Becca puts a hand on my head. "Good cat, I'll get you a treat."

She is a really wonderful person.

We walk back to the table and Kevlar asks, "What was all that?"

Becca answers, "The van is the creep we're after. He has live animals in there. I saw baby gators. Boston says rattlesnakes and flying squirrel too. Got to be what we are here for and that means our information was good. Here, I can show you, I have video." She runs it for them.

She turns to Boston. "Call the rangers, have them stand-by."

"Yeah, that's rattlers," Kevlar says. "Why would someone want to sell rattlesnakes? Can't be much money. And catching them is dangerous. Shoving them in burlap bags is just scary and stupid."

"There is a lucrative market for the venom," Ryan says.

Kevlar looks at Ryan. "Really? Rattlesnake venom?"

"Regulated by the government, but there is a large underground market. The snakes too."

"What now?" Boston asks.

"We watch the van. Organize a takedown for when the buyer shows up," Ryan replied.

"And watch that fat guy by the tent; it's his van," Boston says pointing with her chin.

I nudge Boston for snacks, and she reaches for them, but stops.

"Oops," she says. "I think the buyer just got here. Truck with the camper. Delivers fresh bait to the marina." She stops and then adds, "So you had a reason for asking about bait deliveries."

"Merow?" I nudge the package of Meow Mix with my paw.

You forgot me.

Becca says, "We were not sure. I'll get video." She fiddles with her cell and sets it by Boston's easel. "Come on over to this side Boston and look like you're sketching."

Ryan and Kevlar move over beside Boston to watch the men.

Humph. "Meoww?" I pat the treat package again.

The men from the tent meet the two men getting out of the bait truck. They all look in the van. Talk some. Then start moving burlap bags from the van to the truck. It's kind of funny how they hold them straight out far away from their bodies. They finish with the sacks, and one man, the guy from the tent, climbs into the van.

"Call the Rangers, Boston. We can't wait," Ryan says looking around, "we need to act now."

"Meow???" *Hey! Hungry here.* I bat Boston, and she opens the snacks. She's distracted with her cell, but tips two out on the table.

I pick up one and chew, half listening as she says, "Bob and a couple of squad cars are on their way."

I point my ears at the van. The angry cat is growling. Growling with an accent.

I grab the tidbit and jump down and head for it.

The cat screeches and the guy from the tent hollers

The cat screams again.

I hurry forward, checking back. Boston looks toward the van worried. She knows a cat screech.

A squad car races around the curve and stops behind the two vehicles. Another comes around behind me and blocks the vehicles from the front.

Smart. Humans hunting in a pack again.

The rangers jump out of their vehicles and surround the men by the bait truck.

The van shakes.

A cat's angry yowl growl; a man's anguished scream. More screaming and then the man staggers out of the van, backpedaling. A gun on one hand. A cat stuck on his face.

Wow.

His hands fly up in the air, and the gun goes flying to land near me.

The man is screaming. "Get it off me. Get it off me. My nose. My nose. It's biting my nose off. Ahhh."

He flails around in a circle, trying to pull the cat off. But the animal has both front paws dug in deep around the guy's eyes. Back claws scratching down his neck making deep bloody gouges.

That cat is firmly planted on the guy's face. And she is maaaad.

The guy's screams are almost drowned out by the undulating high pitch of the cat's howling.

Wow. I hope the video is still running.

The cat's teeth, her fangs, are dug deep into the guy's nose.

Ouch. Bet that hurts.

The man topples over near me. I move to the side a step.

The cat digs in one extra time and jumps away, crouching, spitting, and snarling. The man's face is a bloody mess.

Tee hee. Attaboy.

Bob and two rangers approach cautiously. Cautiously because the cat, is between them and the guy. They walk wide around it. The cat ignores them and starts grooming one front paw.

The creep rolls over and reaches for the gun which landed near me. I slap his wrist hard, claws out, and he snatches his hand back with a whine.

Give myself an attaboy. Drew blood. *Teach you to put a cat in a cage.*

The rangers sit the guy up and cuff him. He is bleeding from multiple wounds.

Good.

The ranger ambulance arrives. Timely, because the guy really needs some bandaging.

Boston comes to get me, but I edge away. She starts to grab my leash, but the rangers call her over to the vehicles to look at the animals and ask her what to do.

"Research will want the baby gators. The rattlers? I'd call South Florida Herpetological Society in Miami, have them come to get them. I wouldn't handle the burlap sacks, even to put them in terrariums. Better yet. Call Research, let them deal with all of it."

She introduces Becca and Ryan to the rangers and explains their connection.

"You guys want to take over?" Bob asks Ryan.

"No. You handle it. We are on vacation."

Becca is studying the cat.

"Well," Bob says, "I'm going to take Boston's suggestions and let Research handle the animals. We'll just document the scene. Guard it until they get here. Maybe give this guy some first aid and take the perps to town."

Business done. Boston grabs me.

Darn. That's two times she's grabbed me.

Bob looks over at the cat. "What about that, it is a cat? Right?" he asks. "How did a cat get into the wild-life mix. We don't have domesticated cats in the park do we Boston?"

"No. It might have been left by a camper. It is kind of a rare cat breed," she replies.

Not as rare as Maine Coon cats.

"Do we capture him and hold him for research?"

Boston frowns and tilts her head. "Not sure you want to catch that cat," she says.

"I'll get him," Becca says.

Not a him. Even dirty as she is, she's regal, proud. Almost royal. And angry.

Boston looks at Becca doubtfully.

"What? I made friends with Tiger, didn't I?" Becca says.

She did. And gave me snacks. She's a nice cat person.

"I'll be careful," she says and walks over to stoop in front of the cat. "Can I touch you?" she asks. "You see Tiger. He let me touch his ear. It was soft and silky. I'll bet yours is too. You are a princess."

Princess checks with me, her eyes slitted.

I close and open my eyes in a yes, okay. She watches carefully as Becca reaches out a hand. Strokes an ear. Then slides her hand down Princess's back. "Princess. Your name is Princess. Your title is Princess."

Both kind of sigh. And relax. Friends.

Okay. Boring now. Wait a minute. I left my snacks by the picnic table.

My leash is long enough, and Boston is distracted with Becca and Princess, so I walk over and hunker down by the bag. While I chew, I watch Becca pick Princess up. Crooning to her.

To Boston she says, "She needs a bath."

Both Princess and I stiffen. Boston too.

"No. No, no, no. No bath. You try to wet down that cat and you'll be looking like that guy in the ambulance."

"How do I get her clean then?" Becca asks.

"Rub gently with a dry cloth to get off the surface dirt. Next use a soft brush. You have one?"

Becca nods still stroking Princess.

"And repeat. Dry cloth, brush. You can try a damp cloth for tough parts. Or cotton ball or Q-tip for grime. No bath. She will finish cleaning whatever spots you miss."

"You need help?" Ryan asks standing protectively over Becca.

"I got this," she says and heads back to her camper, whispering to Princess.

"I think you just adopted a cat," Boston tells Ryan.

"Yeah. I did."

"She is a lynx point Siamese which is a Siamese with stripes." Boston tells him. "I'll bring over some cat things in a little while. Food and toys."

What? Where will you get those? Not mine.

"Fish fry tonight," she reminds him as he follows Becca and their new family member.

Boston points a finger at me to let me know she's watching.

I grab another treat before she can take them away.

"Brave smart cat," she says.

105

I am? I am. And should get more treats.

And she gives me two more.

Yay.

"Time to head home and start supper," Kevlar says.

That works.

Back home she goes straight to my toy drawer and takes out one of my toys. "We are going to give this to Princess," she says.

What? You're taking my toys? My toys? No way.

I narrow my eyes.

"Sharing is good."

Sharing is stupid. I don't share.

"But this isn't really sharing."

Right. Not if you take it away from me. Then it isn't mine anymore.

"I know you want her to start her new life with a toy you gave her. She will always be in your debt."

Well, maybe.

"And I will buy you two new toys."

That will work.

But then she goes to the cupboard and takes out a treat package. "For Princess. It's salmon. You don't really like those. And we'll give her the vegan fake turkey can."

That's really gross stuff. I almost feel bad for Princess.

"Both cans. And some kibble."

Are you done? Are you done picking out my stuff and giving it away?

"And for now you can have some fresh redfish for a snack"

Well okay. I let her off the hook and settle down to eat my fish. But still give my tail a couple of sharp jerks.

She is only gone a few minutes, and Kevlar has started frying fish.

A fish fry. My favorite. Fresh caught redfish and hush-puppies. Not real puppies, but fried bread. Boston adds salad fixings, corn on the cob.

Those are not very good. Gross and disgusting.

Kevlar does the cooking for all of us. The Rangers invite themselves after they lock up the bad guys in their own big cage.

Good. I hope they stay there forever.

Bob tells us that Research will decide if the gators are old enough to be on their own; the other animals will be released after it is determined they are healthy. The herpetologist will come and collect the snakes. He will milk the snakes for their venom to make anti-venom.

Not sure how you milk a snake. Funny expression.

Becca says Princess is clean and 'home' and shows us a picture of Princess asleep, on Ryan's pillow. "She's a lynx point Siamese. A rare Siamese," she brags.

Maybe. But not as rare and great as a Maine coon cat.

I get lots of fish both raw and fried. And some shrimp. No tomatoes, no lettuce, no corn.

A happy ending all around.

www.ingramcontent.com/pod-product-compliance
Lightning Source LLC
Chambersburg PA
CBHW041221030426
42336CB00024B/3410